Eat Smart IN MEXICO

How to Decipher the Menu
Know the Market Foods
&
Embark on a Tasting Adventure

Joan Peterson

Illustrated by S.V. Medaris

GINKGO PRESS, INC
Madison, Wisconsin

Eat Smart in Mexico
Joan B. Peterson

Map lettering is by Gail L. Carlson; cover and insert photographs are by Joan Peterson; photograph of Joan Peterson is by Susan Chwae.
The quote by James A. Michener from "This Great Big Wonderful World," from the March 1956 issue of Travel-Holiday Magazine, © 1956 by James A. Michener, is reprinted by permission of the William Morris Agency, LLC, on behalf of the author.

Publisher's Cataloging in Publication
(Prepared by Quality Books Inc.)
Peterson, Joan.
    Eat smart in Mexico : how to decipher the menu, know
the market foods & embark on a tasting adventure / by
Joan Peterson ; illustrated by S.V. Medaris.
    p. cm.
    Includes bibliographical references and index.
    LCCN: 2007908348
    ISBN-13: 978-0-9776801-0-8
    ISBN-10: 0-9776801-0-X

    1. Cookery, Mexican. 2. Diet--Mexico. 3. Food
habits--Mexico. 4. Cookery--Mexico. 5. Mexico--
Guidebooks. 6. Mexico--Description and travel.
I. Title.

TX716.M4P48 2008   641.5972
                      QBI08-600076
Printed in the United States of America

To Brook

Wordsmith, colleague, friend
and foodie-in-the-making

Contents

The Cuisine of Mexico　　1

An historical survey of the development of Mexico's mestizo cuisine, a rich amalgamation of the foods of pre-Columbian agriculturalists and the Spanish and other Europeans.

Regional Mexican Food　　17

A quick tour through the six regions of Mexico to see the diversity of cooking styles encountered in traveling the length and breadth of the country.

Tastes of Mexico　　37

A selection of delicious, easy-to-prepare regional and national recipes provided by well-known food professionals. Try them before leaving home.

Shopping in Mexico's Food Markets   59

Tips to increase your savvy in both the exciting outdoor food markets and modern supermarkets.

Resources   61

A listing of stores carrying hard-to-find Mexican foods and of groups that focus on travel to Mexico or offer opportunities for person-to-person contact through home visits to gain a deeper understanding of the country, including its cuisine.

Helpful Phrases   65

Questions in Spanish, with English translations, which will assist you in finding, ordering and buying foods or ingredients, particularly regional specialties.

Menu Guide   69

An extensive listing of menu entries in Spanish, with English translations, to make ordering food an easy and immediately rewarding experience.

Foods and Flavors Guide   101

A comprehensive glossary of ingredients, kitchen utensils and cooking methods in Spanish, with English translations.

Preface

> If you reject the food, ignore the customs, fear the
> religion and avoid the people, you might better
> stay home. You are like a pebble thrown into
> water; you become wet on the surface but you are
> never a part of the water.
>
> —JAMES A. MICHENER

As an inveterate traveler, I have had many adventures around the world. I have traveled independently, relying on my own research and resources. One way I gauge the success of my trips is how well I become familiar with the native cuisine. To me, there is no more satisfying way to become immersed in a new culture than to mingle with the local people in the places where they enjoy good food and conversation, in their favorite neighborhood cafés, restaurants, picnic spots or outdoor markets. I try to capture the essence of a country through its food, and seek out unfamiliar ingredients and preparations that provide scrumptious new tastes. By meandering on foot or navigating on local buses, I have discovered serendipitously many memorable eating establishments away from more heavily trafficked tourist areas. As an unexpected but cherished diner, I have had the pleasure of seeing my efforts in learning the cuisine appreciated by the people in ways that make an understanding of each other's language unimportant.

Each trip energizes me as though it were my first; the preparation for a visit becomes almost as exciting as the trip itself. Once I determine the destination, I begin to accumulate information—buying most, if not all, the current, relevant guide books, raiding the libraries and sifting through my hefty collection of travel articles and clippings for useful data. A high priority for me is the creation of a reference list of the foods, with translations, from the gathered resource materials. For all but a handful of popular European destinations, however, the amount of information devoted to food is limited. General travel guides and phrase books contain only an overview of the cuisine because they cover so many other subjects of interest to travelers. Not surprisingly, the reference lists I have compiled from these sources have been incomplete; many items on menus were unrecognizable. Of course, some menus have translations but these often are more amusing than helpful, and many waiters cannot provide further assistance in interpreting them. Furthermore, small neighborhood establishments—some of my favorite dining spots—frequently lack printed menus and, instead, post their daily offerings, typically in the native language, on chalkboards outside the door. So unless you are adequately familiar with the language of food, you may pass up good tasting experiences!

To make dining a more satisfying cultural experience for myself and for others, I resolved on an earlier trip to improve upon the reference lists I always compiled and research the food "on the spot" throughout my next trip. Upon my return, I would generate a more comprehensive guide, making it easier for future travelers to know the cuisine. The book that resulted from that "next trip" featured the cuisine of Brazil and represented the first in what became a series of in-depth explorations of the foods of foreign countries. To date eight other EAT SMART guides have been published. These explore the cuisines of Turkey, Indonesia, Mexico, Poland, Morocco, India, Peru and Sicily. The guides for Brazil, Turkey and now Mexico are in their second editions. My intention is to enable the traveler to decipher the menu with confidence and shop or browse in the supermarkets and in the fascinating, lively outdoor food and spice markets with greater knowledge.

My own journeys have been greatly enhanced because I have sampled unfamiliar foods. One of many illustrations of this in Mexico occurred in Pátzcuaro, a serene colonial city in the Lakeland region of Michoacán, high in the Central Sierras. This is the land of the Purépecha people, or Tarascans, as the Spanish called them.

Many tourists visit Pátzcuaro, and the island of Janitzio in nearby Lake Pátzcuaro, during the annual celebrations for The Day of the Dead on November 1–2. They come to see the spectacular parade of boats and canoes headed for Janitzio, laden with offerings of special bread (*pan de muerto*), fruits and candies for the dead. These will be carried along a path emblazoned with candlelight to grave sites in the hilltop cemetery. I came to

Pátzcuaro, however, to sample the cuisine. Bruce Kraig and Dudley Nieto, in their book, *Cuisines of Hidden Mexico,* raved so about the food of Michoacán and the charms of Pátzcuaro that I added a stop to this city on my jaunt around the country.

The two Margaritas, as I call them, of Pátzcuaro's Doña Paca Café gave me a delicious survey of the area's cuisine. Margarita Arriaga owns Mansión Iturbe, a grand 17th-century mansion that was given as a dowry to her great grandmother and that now serves as a bed and breakfast hotel. Doña Paca Café is the hotel's restaurant. Daughter Margarita Pedraza handles public relations for her mother. Both see that a fine selection of authentic regional dishes of Michoacán are showcased in their restaurant.

My introduction to the food began within minutes of our arrival. Mother and daughter joined me in the dining room as the dishes I was to sample began to appear. Between bites I learned their composition and history. Highlights included a classic dish for Purépecha fiestas, *churipo,* which is a beef and vegetable stew flavored with the herb called *epazote* and a sour cactus fruit called *xoconostle.* Plain *corundas,* the irregular-shaped *tamales* wrapped in long green corn leaves, accompany the dish as bread. *Sopa* Tarasca (Tarascan soup), one of the specialty dishes of Pátzcuaro, is a rich blend of *ancho* and *guajillo* chiles, tomatoes, beans and pieces of *tortillas,* topped with cream and crumbled Cotija cheese. Lake Pátzcuaro provides staple menu items: *querepo,* small whitefish fried and eaten whole, served with a tomatillo-based sauce, and *charales,* tiny sun-dried fish served fried.

Fully stuffed, all of us then set out to explore the food selections of the night street market. We had room for small samples of exotic black ice cream made from the pulp of the black sapodilla fruit (*zapote negro*) and rich, orange-colored ice cream made from the pulp of the *mamey.* This was followed by some hearty *atole de grano,* a warm drink of *masa,* or corn dough, and fresh corn, flavored and colored light green with wild anise.

Next morning, again gathered around the dining table, I continued my research, and sampled breakfast dishes. I had been in Pátzcuaro for less than a day, and had already eaten my way through what must have been over several weeks' worth of meals. I was unable to sample the traditional dish of Michoacán (*uchepos*) made of fresh corn *tamales* wrapped in green corn husks, but I will be back when they are in season!

The purpose of our EAT SMART guides is to encourage sampling new and unusual foods. What better way is there to get to know a culture than through its cuisine? Informed travelers, I know, will be more open to experimentation. The guides also will help steer the traveler away from foods they want to avoid—everyone confesses to disliking something!

This guide has four main chapters. The first provides a history of Mexican cuisine. It is followed by a chapter with descriptions of regional Mexican foods. The other main chapters are extensive listings, placed near the end of the book for easy reference. The first is an alphabetical compilation of menu entries, including more general Mexican fare as well as regional specialties. Some noteworthy, not-to-be-missed dishes with country-wide popularity are labeled "national favorite" in the margin next to the menu entry. Some classic regional dishes of Mexico—also not to be missed—are labeled "regional classic." The second list contains a translation of food items and terms associated with preparing and serving food. This glossary will be useful in interpreting menus since it is impractical to cover in the *Menu Guide* all the flavors or combinations possible for certain dishes.

Also included in the book is a chapter offering hints on browsing and shopping in the food markets and one with phrases that will be useful in restaurants and food markets to learn more about the foods of Mexico. A chapter is devoted to Mexican recipes. Do take time to experiment with these recipes before departure; it is a wonderful and immediately rewarding way to preview Mexican food. Most special Mexican ingredients in these recipes can be obtained in the United States; substitutions for unavailable ingredients are given. Sources for hard-to-find Mexican ingredients can be found in the *Resources* chapter, which also cites some groups that focus on travel to Mexico to experience the food or offer the opportunity to have person-to-person contact through home visits to gain a deeper understanding of the country, including its cuisine.

I call your attention to the form at the end of the book. It can be used to order additional copies of this book as well as the other culinary guidebooks in the EAT SMART series directly from Ginkgo Press.

¡buen viaje y buen provecho!

JOAN PETERSON
Madison, Wisconsin

Acknowledgments

I gratefully acknowledge those who assisted me in preparing this book. Ruben Medina, Department of Spanish and Portuguese, University of Wisconsin–Madison, for translations; Margarita Arriaga, Rick Bayless, María Luisa Enríquez Enríquez, Mariana Franco, Lucinda Hutson, Diana Kennedy, W. Park Kerr, Bruce Kraig, Rachel Laudan, Zarela Martínez, Timothy Mello, Elisabeth Lambert Ortiz, Maricel Presilla, Patricia Quintana, Mary Stec, Marilyn Tausend, Susana Trilling, Joseph Wrede and Nancy Zaslavsky for contributing recipes; Susie V. Medaris for her magical illustrations; Gail Carlson for enlivening the maps with her handwriting; Susan Chwae (Ginkgo Press) for a knockout cover design; Lanita Haag (Widen Enterprises) for the excellent four-color separations; Susan Chwae for the photograph of Joan Peterson; and Nicol Knappen (Ekeby) for bringing the text neatly to order.

I am indebted to many people for help in identifying regional Mexican foods and menu items, or providing source material. Thanks to Phil Crossley, Department of Geography, University of Texas, Austin; Hugh H. Iltis, Professor Emeritus, Department of Botany, University of Wisconsin–Madison; Bruce Kraig, Department of History, Roosevelt University, Chicago, H. Bradley Shaffer, Department of Evolution and Ecology, University of California, Davis; Marilyn Tausend, Culinary Adventures and Ron Cooper, President, Del Maguey, Ltd. Co., Single Village Mezcal; and in Mexico, Diana Kennedy, Michoacán, Patricia Quintana, Mexico City and Susana Trilling, Oaxaca. Thanks also to Hugh H. Iltis, Professor Emeritus, Department of Botany, University of Wisconsin–Madison and Ron Cooper, President, Del Maguey, Ltd. Co., Single Village Mezcal for illustration materials.

I'd like to thank the following people for introducing me to regional foods or presenting cooking demonstrations in Mexico: Margarita Arriaga and Margarita Pedraza, owners, Doña Paca Café and Mansión Iturbe, Pátzcuaro, Michoacán, Jesús Palacios B., Toluca, Mexico, Raul Rosado Lixa, Mérida, Yucatán, owner, El Anfitrón restaurant, Patricia Quintana, chef, cookbook author and teacher, Mexico City, Terry Dana, International Travel Group, Mexico City, J. Antonío Iñiguez, Guadalajara, Jalisco, Susana Trilling, author and owner, Seasons of My Heart Cooking School, Oaxaca, María Luisa Enríquez Enríquez, teacher, Las Chinas de Puebla restaurant cooking school, Puebla, and her assistants, Antonia Garcia de la Rosa and María del Rocio Pérez Jiménez, Marilyn Tausend, cookbook author and President, Culinary Adventures, Inc., Gig Harbor, Washington, Carmen Barnard, Morelia, Michoacán, culinary educator and Mexico coordinator, Culinary Adventures, Inc. and Diana Kennedy, Zitácuaro, Michoacán, cookbook author and teacher, Culinary Adventures, Inc.

I also am indebted to Diana Kennedy for critically reading the first edition. Her suggestions have been incorporated into this edition.

And special thanks to Brook Soltvedt, a most perceptive and helpful editor.

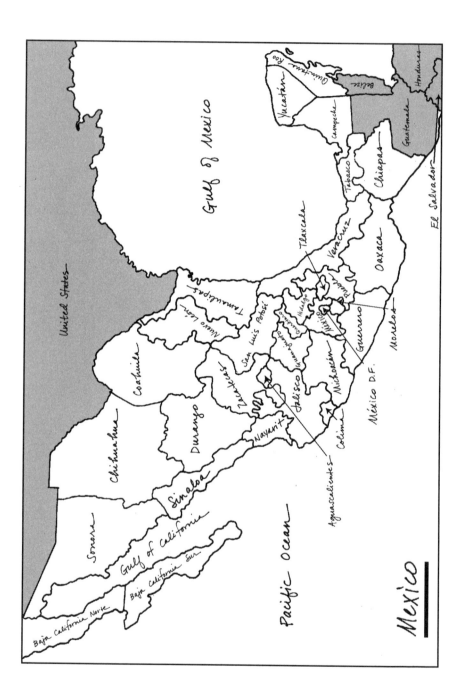

Mexico

The Cuisine of Mexico

An Historical Survey

Many of the world's most important food plants—corn, tomato, squash, *cacao,* tomatillo, avocado, pumpkin, bean, sweet potato, vanilla and chile— were domesticated in Mexico and were foods unknown to the pre-Columbian Old World. Imagining menus without them certainly is difficult. It seems apt that the geographic outlines of Mexico define a cornucopia, the symbol of plenty.

Early History

The ancestors of Mexico's earliest people migrated to the New World from Siberia 20,000–50,000 years ago to find new habitats. The passage of these first Americans was made possible during the Ice Age by a natural land corridor connecting Siberia and Alaska, which became exposed when the sea level fell during a period of maximal glaciation.

The immigrant hunters and foragers followed their food source—herds of large grazing beasts such as the bison, mastodon, and woolly mammoth— across the bridge from Asia. They survived for most of the year on meat, which they cooked over a fire or dried in the sun. Some of the dried meat was pulverized and mixed with suet and dried berries, and then pressed into cakes that resisted spoilage for long periods of time.

In continuous pursuit of prey, small bands of arctic hunters gradually moved south and found a more hospitable climate and greater variety of plant life. It is not known when the first people arrived in Mexico but evidence from radiocarbon dating has determined a human presence in the fertile, centrally located Valley of Mexico by about 20,000 BC.

Seasonally nomadic occupants of caves in nearby Tehuacán Valley, a desert region southeast of Mexico City, left well-preserved animal and plant remains from which much has been learned about early food habits and the transition from plant collection to cultivation. By about 6800 BC, most of the large herbivores had become extinct, either through overhunting or as a consequence of the rise in temperature at the end of the Ice Age. Primarily small game such as squirrels, rabbits, rodents, birds and snakes were eaten now. Antelope and horses were not yet extinct. Fruits, berries, nuts, leaves and roots became more important in the diet. Primitive tools such as the stone mortar (*molcajete*) and pestle (*tejolote*) were used to crush wild seeds.

By 6500 BC, several plants had been domesticated: first bottle gourds, then pumpkins, chiles, beans and squash. The all-important corn plant, domesticated around 5000 BC, had pencil-thin, inch-long ears. Over the next several millennia, plants with larger ears bearing many more kernels would evolve, and by propagating these higher-yielding plants, farmers became more self-sufficient. Corn stalks also provided food. They were chewed to extract their nourishing sugary juices. Interestingly, corn's origin is still speculative; the plant is only found under cultivation. A current theory is that it arose from a tall, wild grass called teosinte, whose stems were also chewed to obtain sweet juice.

Cotton, avocado, and amaranth were cultivated by 2500 BC. Cotton fibers and those from the agave plant (*maguey*) were used for weaving. Quids of the roasted base of agave leaves were chewed to extract the juices, then discarded. The juice was also drawn from the plant and drunk fresh (*aguamiel*) or naturally fermented (*pulque*). Kitchens were equipped with clay crockery.

Permanently settled villages appeared about 1500 BC as agriculture became more important, and an adequate food supply could be produced. There was a greater reliance on plants for dietary protein because there were few domesticated animals. By this time dogs had been tamed, but it would be another several hundred years before the turkey was domesticated, and not until the arrival of the Spanish in the early 1500s would pigs, sheep, goats, cattle, horses and chickens be in the barnyard.

Corn became more nutritious with the development of the process called *nixtamalization,* whereby corn is pretreated with lime, either from wood ashes or limestone. The earliest recorded use of lime in ancient kitchens is about 100 BC. Lime-coated cooking pots were found in Teotihuacán, the first great metropolis in central Mexico. Dried corn kernels were heated in limewater, which frees certain essential amino acids and the vitamin niacin from normally indigestible parts of the grain. It also softens the kernel's tough hull, making it easier to remove. Treated corn made a more flexible

Experimental strains of corn produced by crossing popcorn and teosinte, a wild grass thought to be the ancestor of corn. Through a series of crossings and selections for small ears, one can produce ears that resemble what the oldest ears of corn might have looked like. Shown here at approximately 80% of full size, the two ears with a central spike (left) are considered the equivalent of corn 4,500 years old; the ear with no central spike (right) the equivalent of corn 3,500–4,000 years old. Drawn from hybrids raised by Nobel laureate George Beadle in the 1970s, provided by Dr. Hugh H. Iltis, Emeritus Professor of Botany at the University of Wisconsin.

and nutritious dough (*masa*). Now a diet of corn and beans could provide the proper balance of amino acids to meet the daily protein requirement. The importance of these vegetables and squash was evident in the layout of the *milpa,* or cornfield. Early farmers planted small, repeating patches with beans planted next to corn, to twine about the stalk for support, and squash planted in a circle around them.

The Olmecs

By about 1200 BC, the first of Mexico's ancient civilizations emerged in the humid, sweltering Gulf Coast region in present-day Veracruz and Tabasco, an area of abundant rivers, lakes and marshes. The people of this "mother culture," the Olmecs, developed a complex society with a hereditary elite. They had a well-developed religious institution and built pyramids for use as temples, grouping them in ceremonial centers for the worship of their deities. Among their intellectual achievements were the development of a hieroglyphic writing system and a calendar. Excellent carvers, they created astounding monolithic heads from basalt to honor their leaders. Subsequent cultures in Mesoamerica—the term anthropologists use for the area of central Mexico and parts of Central America that were civilized when the Spanish conquistadors arrived—profited immensely from their rich heritage.

The basic crop of Olmec farmers was corn. Other vegetables produced were beans, squash and chiles. They also cultivated the *cacao* tree, whose pods produced the much-coveted seeds for making chocolate. Their diet included an abundance of fish, especially the snook. Menus also included shellfish, aquatic birds, deer, turtle, and the domesticated dog and turkey. Drinking water was provided by a system of buried drains serving as aqueducts.

The culture flourished until about 400 BC. It came to an abrupt and violent end as evidenced by systematic and deliberate destruction of monuments and sculptures, either by their own hand or an invasion, or both.

The Maya

By the time the Olmec culture came to an end, the Maya had already settled in villages along the Pacific coastal plain of southeastern Mexico, and continuing south into Guatemala and Honduras. The Maya civilization can be traced back to about 1500 BC. It evolved slowly, flourishing between 600–900 AD. By this time it extended from the Yucatán Peninsula west to Tabasco and Chiapas, and into Guatemala, Belize, and western Honduras and El Salvador. It was a diverse geographic area with climatic variations ranging from dry plains to tropical forests.

The Maya civilization would be the greatest of all in Mesoamerica. The Maya made remarkable achievements in astronomy and mathematics, and devised a calendar by which they could calculate solar events with great precision. A system of hieroglyphics was developed to put all their words in writing. No other Mesoamerican cultures reached this level of literacy.

The Maya civilization was organized into city-states controlled by ruling dynasties. At their core was a ceremonial center with pyramids and multi-roomed palaces, the civic seat of political, social and religious activity. These urban complexes were not true cities, however. Other than rulers and those with noble lineage, who lived near the ceremonial centers, the bulk of the population was dispersed in the surrounding area in hamlets.

The basis of the economy was agriculture and corn was the mainstay. A labor force of farmers living in such hamlets grew corn, beans, squash, tomatoes and chiles in land that typically was burned before it was seeded because there were no draft animals to pull plows to till the soil. Slash and burn farming depletes the soil after a few years, however. It has to lie fallow for several growing seasons to regain fertility. Thus there was a continual need to farm new land to sustain the growing community. To make better use of land unsuitable for farming, raised fields of piled dirt (*chinampas,* see also p. 8) were built in marshlands, and steep slopes were terraced. Canals and reservoirs were constructed to help control the water supply. Some urban complexes in the Yucatán were constructed near *cenotes,* subterranean fresh water systems within the porous limestone shelf, providing a supply of water for drinking and for crops.

Root crops such as manioc and sweet potatoes were grown in the lowlands, and in coastal settlements there were fish, shellfish and turtles. Fruits included

Artist's rendition of Yum Kaax (left), the Maya god of corn. He usually is depicted with a headdress made of a stylized corn plant or an ear of corn. On the right are (top to bottom) the name glyph of the corn god, the glyph for corn seed and the glyph for an ear of corn.

the coconut, papaya and breadnut. Dogs, turkeys and rabbits provided animal protein.

In certain inland regions and the Pacific coastal plain, *cacao* trees were cultivated for chocolate. Painted ceramic vessels found in burial sites of rulers depicted the method of creating a foamy head as the beverage was poured into a vessel from one held high above it. *Cacao* beans were so important that the Maya used them as coinage, a use also employed centuries later by the Aztecs in central Mexico.

The Maya believed in many gods. Not surprisingly, their pantheon included a god of corn, Yum Kaax. He was a principal but powerless god; his fate was controlled by interplay between the death god (Yum Cimil), who could bring drought, and the rain god (Chac). So important was corn that the Maya believed their ancestors were created out of corn cobs, the substance the gods had used to mold into a human being after failing with wood. The gods were happy with the humans made of corn because they were more intelligent and grateful to their creators than the people made of wood.

About 900 AD the Maya civilization began to decline. Historians speculate that pestilence and population pressure led to agricultural collapse. Over the next several centuries, outside groups infiltrated the Maya territory, especially in northern Yucatán, and for much of the time before the Spanish Conquest the Maya were ruled by others.

Information on Maya food habits in the early 1500s is obtained from accounts written by Spaniards, including Hernán Cortés, who on preliminary explorations of the Yucatán encountered and dined with the native people. They wrote about the cooked gruel (*atole*) and uncooked gruel (*pozol*) made of ground corn mixed with water, often sweetened with honey or flavored with ground chiles. They ate *tamales* and *tortillas* made of *nixtamal,* manioc bread, roasted turkeys and orchard-grown fruits such as papaya, pineapples, *zapote, chicozapote* and cactus fruits. *Cacao* trees, not readily adapted to growing in dry areas of the Yucatán, were cleverly planted in *cenotes,* but no chocolate beverages were offered to the Spaniards. Descriptions of late sixteenth-century Maya meals come from the Franciscan Diego de Landa, who became bishop of Yucatán in 1572, and others. Menu items included small black beans, *pinole,* a drink of powdered, toasted corn, and chocolate. The chocolate was drunk plain, with *pinole,* or stained brick-red with *achiote,* the small red seeds of the annatto tree. *Masa* for *tamales* and *tortillas* was mixed with ground chiles. The *tamales* could be stuffed with black beans, ground, toasted squash seeds, squash flowers and greens such as *chilipín* (*chepil*), *chaya* and purslane. *Tortillas* were eaten with sauces made of chiles and ground, toasted squash seeds, flavored with the herb called *epazote*. Meat included iguana, deer, peccary (wild pig), dog, monkey and armadillo, and a *pib,* or pit-oven, was in use. Fish and shellfish were also eaten, but they, along with meat, were foods primarily of the elite.

The Aztecs

In the mid 1200s the Aztecs, or Mexica as they called themselves, arrived in the Valley of Mexico, a highland area of about 2,500 square miles some 7,200 feet above sea level in central Mexico. There was within the Valley at that time a large, shallow lake, the site of present-day Mexico City.

Tamales, a popular food of ancient and modern Mexico. *Masa,* or corn dough, is blended with lard until light, and steamed in a wrapper of corn husks or banana leaves (top left). The corn often used is *cacahuazintle,* a large-kerneled white corn also used to make hominy. Drawn from *Mexico's Feasts of Life,* by Patricia Quintana.

Permanent Aztec settlement was delayed for about another 75 years. These savage newcomers were repeatedly expelled for squatting on the land of more civilized inhabitants of the Valley, who lived in city-states surrounding the lake. The banished Aztecs finally called home a swampy, uninhabited island in the lake. They named their city "Tenochtitlán" or "Place of the Prickly-Pear Cactus Fruit," evidently fulfilling the tribal prophecy that they end their odyssey and construct a city where they see an eagle perched on a cactus.

Through their prowess as mercenaries and a series of clever alliances, the Aztecs emerged as the most powerful group in the Valley. They began a long series of conquests and consolidations, and by 1500 the empire they ruled included most of central and southern Mexico. The conquered enemy lands were not subsequently occupied and became the source of vast tribute.

When the Spanish under Hernán Cortés first arrived in the Valley of Mexico in 1519, they were transfixed by the magnificent metropolis of Tenochtitlán, with its complex of ceremonial temples, palaces, and administrative buildings, its canals, its huge markets and the three causeways interconnecting the island and mainland. From Spanish chroniclers of the sixteenth century we have abundant written accounts of the everyday activities and the last days of existence of the great Aztec Empire and its ruler, Emperor Moctezuma (called Montezuma by the Spanish). These early historians and ethnographers include Bernal Díaz del Castillo, one of the Spanish soldiers commanded by Hernán Cortés, missionaries such as Friars Bernardino de Sahagún and Diego Durán, and Cortés himself. Sahagún's accounts of culinary matters are wonderfully detailed. We are also able to learn from the Aztecs, who recorded their history, sometimes embellished, in codices, or pictoral records.

At the time the Spanish arrived in the Valley, the city's population stood at about 200,000. To feed this many mouths, Aztec farmers used a system of wetland agriculture devised by earlier cultures, but increased its capacity. They made fertile, raised "floating" beds of sludge and aquatic vegetation dug up from the lakes's bottom and held this reclaimed soil in place with stakes. These well-irrigated, year-round garden strips, or *chinampas,* were separated by canals and produced a main crop—corn—in addition to beans, squash, chiles, pumpkins, tomatoes, tomatillos, greens (*quelites*), amaranth, seeds from a species of plant in the sage family (*chia*) used to make a drink, herbs such as *epazote* and flowers. Land unsuitable for irrigation was farmed for a few years and then allowed to lie fallow for several growing seasons until it became productive again. Steep hillsides were terraced. Additional food supplies—amounting to tons of corn, amaranth, *chia* and beans—came to the city each year as tribute from the conquered provinces.

The lake and marshes provided fish, frogs, tadpoles, small shrimp and waterfowl. Some of the more interesting aquatic protein sources were worms, axolotls (larval salamanders), water flies, including their eggs and nests, and a protein-rich blue-green alga, *Spirulina,* which was scraped off the water surface and pressed into biscuits. This nutritious alga is available today in health food stores, and is touted as a high-energy and vitamin-rich supplement, especially beneficial to vegetarians.

Game included rabbit, deer, peccary (wild pig), armadillo, iguana and birds, but meat was rarely eaten by ordinary people. Of the two domesticated animals, dog was less desirable than turkey. Some fruits and vegetables in the Aztec diet were plums, *capulín, tejocote, cherimoyas, zapotes,* sweet potatoes, jicama, avocados, manioc, squash flowers and purslane.

Agave plants (*maguey*), already known to earlier Mexican cultures, were grown on non-irrigated soil on the surrounding hillsides. The fermented juice of this plant (*pulque*) was used for religious ceremonies. There were strict laws against drunkenness, however, and offenders faced death. No more than four cups were allowed at a feast, although consumption by the elderly was less restricted. The short, wide stem of the plant and the base of its spiked leaves were roasted, and quids were chewed to extract the sweet

juice. Worms burrowing in the plant were also eaten. Today such worms find their way into bottles of *mezcal.* The nopal cactus was also cultivated. Its fruit (*tuna*) and succulent leaves, or paddles, were important edibles. In periods of drought these plants were reliable food sources.

The Aztec kitchen was equipped with a three-legged, sloped grindstone (*metate*) for crushing *nixtamalized* corn and a stone mortar (*molcajete*) and pestle (*tejolote*) for grinding seeds, spices, chiles and other sauce components. Foods were grilled on a round ceramic griddle (*comal*).

The three-legged basalt mortar (*molcajete*) and pestle (*tejolote*) used to grind spices and chiles for sauces. The mortar typically becomes a serving bowl for the sauces made in it.

Agave plant (*Agave tequilana*) used for the production of *tequila*. The plant's pineapple-like heart, or *piña,* that which is left after the spiked leaves, or *pencas,* are chopped off, is cut into pieces and roasted. The juice obtained by pressing cooked pieces of the heart is fermented and then distilled, a process introduced by the Spanish. The hub of *tequila* production is Tequila, Jalisco.

Because there were no fatty animals for the production of grease and oil, food was not fried. Common cooking vessels were two-handled, round-bottomed clay pots (*ollas*).

The beverage of the masses was water. Chocolate was the prestige drink reserved for the elite, priests, warriors and the merchants who trafficked in goods from distant provinces. Those forbidden to savor chocolate were killed if caught breaking the rules. *Cacao* beans had to be transported from the tropical lowlands where the trees were cultivated, a great distance from Tenochtitlán. Fermented, roasted beans were ground, dissolved in water and enjoyed cold, with a frothy head. Sometimes ground corn or chiles were added. Honey was used for sweetness, often with vanilla.

Corn was the daily sustenance and the focus of important religious rites. It was consumed principally in the form of *tamales, tortillas* and *atole,* a gruel or drink made with ground corn mixed with honey or chiles. *Tortillas* varied in texture, thickness, size and color. The affluent had theirs served in baskets, nicely wrapped in cotton cloth to keep warm. *Tamales* and *tortillas* for the average person were plain or filled with beans, with some chile sauce for flavor. Those of higher social status had fillings of fruits, fish or meat and more complex sauces of tomatoes, chiles and ground squash seeds. They also had elaborate casseroles.

Emperor Moctezuma dined amidst great plenty. He reportedly selected his meal from over 300 dishes presented to him at mealtime. The meat selections alone included preparations of rabbit, turkey, duck, venison, peccary and many types of birds. After dining he drank his frothy chocolate from a solid gold vessel.

Amaranth seeds played an important role in the annual feast day celebration of Huitzilopochtli, the Aztecs' tribal diety, who was god of the sun and war. A mixture of seeds, pulverized corn and honey or blood from sacrificial victims was molded into idols of the god, which were ceremonially consumed. The Spanish were appalled at what they considered a sacrilege and banned the production of amaranth after the Conquest.

The principal marketplace was enormous, accommodating over 60,000 buyers and sellers daily. Its grandeur surpassed all the Spaniards knew in the Old World. Both foodstuffs and non-edible items were marketed, many brought by merchants from every province of the Empire, and all neatly arranged in stalls by category. Each was then subdivided by place of origin so buyers would know where things were cultivated or obtained. Hungry shoppers also had a wide variety of prepared foods to eat. *Cacao* beans and transparent quills filled with gold particles served as currency.

The Spanish

The end of Mesoamerican civilization occurred on August 13, 1521. Cortés laid naval seige to Tenochtitlán some three months earlier and when the Aztecs refused to surrender, the city was demolished, building by building. Already weakened by a smallpox epidemic spread by the foreigners, the natives held on for 80 days before the end came. Retribution at the hands of the Aztecs' many enemies, who had allied themselves with Cortés, sealed the horrible fate of the once-proud city and its inhabitants.

After defeating the Aztecs, Cortés and his followers built a new city upon the ruins, and the colonial period of New Spain began. Within a few years they established Spanish hegemony over the former Aztec Empire, and as the population of Spaniards in Mexico grew, so did the expansion of Spanish-dominated territory. Fearful that Cortés would not be responsible to the Spanish king, the Crown made him the Marqués del Valle de Oaxaca and sent a nobleman to rule as viceroy.

The Spanish conquerors, now settlers, had not learned to like native staples. They wanted to raise herds of familiar animals and grow the crops of the Old World. It was wheat they wanted, and wine and olive oil.

The New and Old Worlds were beginning to experience the "Columbian Exchange" of plants and animals. The Spanish brought pigs, cattle, sheep, goats, horses and chickens on early voyages. They also brought their beloved grains—wheat, rice and barley—and introduced many fruits and vegetables such as onions, garlic, garbanzo beans, carrots, turnips, spinach, peaches, pears, grapes, citrus fruits, bananas and sugar cane.

Large herds of cattle roamed extensive tracts of land as ranching spread to the grasslands of northern Mexico, which were ideally suited for it. Within

One of Spain's greatest gifts to Mexican cuisine, the pig is prepared innumerable ways. Among the more popular are *carnitas,* juicy pieces of meat and offal deep-fried in lard, and *chicharrón,* a crispy snack made by boiling scored pork rind in lard.

30 years of the fall of Tenochtitlán, meat was so plentiful that colonists had more of it than they could eat. Although the subjugated Indians were initially kept from owning large domestic animals, for fear of an uprising, they readily accepted the new animal foods. Corn, however, still dominated their diet.

Pork fat, or lard, was used by the Spanish as a reasonable substitute for olive oil. It would alter many pre-Conquest dishes, as would sugar. Milk, cream and cheese, the by-products of a thriving cattle industry, became abundant, as did chicken eggs.

Wheat was a high-priority food to the colonists. Along with meat, it was an inescapable part of their culture. Wherever new cities were built, the success of each project was in good measure based on how self-sufficient the colonists were in supplying this precious commodity to sustain them.

From records kept by the town fathers concerning food supplies, prices and merchant honesty, we know some of the food that was on early colonial plates. *Empanadas* filled with meat, fish and fowl were eaten. Local lake fish and imported dried fish were used. These pastries were also filled with finely shredded chicken breasts cooked in milk, sugar and flour. For the sweet tooth to munch on there were candied fruits, vegetables, nuts and squash seeds, an early use of one of the indigenous vegetables.

Chocolate was the first native food accepted by Mexico's noble Spanish population. We know it was drunk in 1534 as a prelude to elegant banquets hosted by Antonio de Mendoza, the first viceroy of New Spain, and Hernán Cortés, Marqués del Valle de Oaxaca, to celebrate the signing of peace treaties between Spain and France.

Spanish goods shipped to the territory of New Spain arrived at Veracruz, her first port city. They were brought by mule trains to Mexico City, the capital of the viceroyalty. The need for an intermediate outpost prompted the construction in 1531 of the city of Puebla, which became renowned for its preeminence in convent cooking.

From the beginning of Spanish colonization, the Catholic church labored to convert the natives to Christianity. Monks and nuns provided religious training and helped protect Indians' rights. Aside from their religious mission, nuns devoted much energy to gastronomy as a way to finance their church activities. They continued their Old World tradition of making preserves, sweets and confections. This fondness for rich, sweet desserts was inherited from the Moors who had occupied Spain for several centuries. In 1608, the Santa Rosa convent was founded in Puebla and its sisters are said to have created the famous sauce, *mole* Poblano, which fused the native

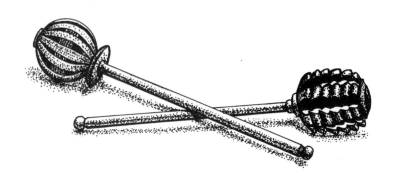

Molinillos, hand-carved wooden beaters used to make a thick layer of foam on top of hot chocolate. They were a Spanish contribution to the Mexican kitchen. Drawn from *The True History of Chocolate,* by Sophie D. Coe.

elements of chiles and chocolate with Old World ingredients such as spices, garlic, onions and sugar.

Mestizo culinary tradition began in earnest in early colonial kitchens with native cooks. Less-affluent Spaniards married native women, who began creating dishes that combined ancient indigenous ways and ingredients with foods from the Old World. Another amalgamation of cultures occurred in these colonial kitchens. Native utensils such as the mortar (*molcajete*) and pestle (*tejolote*), gourds and the grinding stone (*metate*) with its narrow stone roller (*metlapil,* or *mano*), were joined by European strainers, flour sieves, graters and colanders. Hot chocolate was stirred with a Spanish, hand-carved wooden beater (*molinillo*) to make a thick layer of foam on top.

The French

The colonial era lasted 300 years. Independence was won from Spain in 1821 and Mexican borders were opened to the people, products and culinary arts of other nations. International flavors added further depth to the rich Mexican cuisine. The French, who briefly occupied Mexico from 1864 to 1867 under Maximilian of Hapsburg, introduced to the country several French, Austro-Hungarian and Italian dishes. The Emperor and his wife,

Empress Carlota, preferred their European cuisine and brought with them a cooking staff headed by a Hungarian-born chef to make these foods. Among the lasting culinary additions from this era were cakes, crêpes and the small, oblong, split-topped bread roll known as the *bolillo*. Interestingly, one of the most desired fillings for crêpes is *cuitlacoche,* a black corn fungus that was a prized food of the Aztecs.

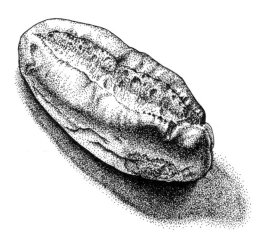

Bolillo, a small, oblong bread roll with a characteristic lengthwise score on top. A longer version of this French contribution to Mexican cuisine is called *pan* Francés in the Yucatán.

In modern times culinary professionals in Mexico are trying to call attention to the the rich heritage of mestizo cuisine so that the traditional dishes are not overshadowed by foreign contributions much in vogue in the culinary repertoire. Travelers to Mexico are finding a resurgence in delicious regional offerings on menus.

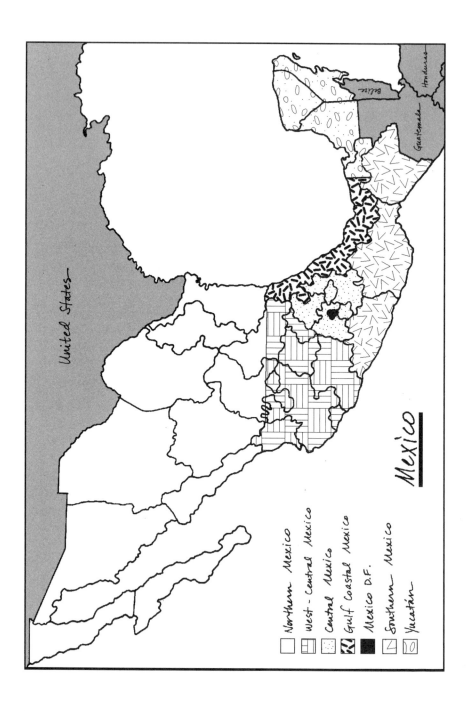

Mexico

Northern Mexico
West - Central Mexico
Central Mexico
Gulf Coastal Mexico
Mexico D.F.
Southern Mexico
Yucatán

United States

Belize

Guatemala

Honduras

Regional Mexican Food

A Quick Tour of Mexican Foods and Their Regional Variations

Mexican Food in a Nutshell

Mexico's mestizo cuisine is a rich amalgamation of the foods of pre-Columbian agriculturalists and the many altogether different ones imported from abroad to sustain the Spanish conquistadors. When both cultures met head-on in the New World in the early 1500s, neither was inclined to significantly alter its traditional diet. The Indian staff of life was corn, but it was unappealing to the Spaniards, who thought this large-seeded grass inferior to wheat, their basic carbohydrate staple. Both Mesoamerican and Spanish food traditions, however, survived the collision of their respective kitchens. Tastes diversified, aided by intermarriage. In the four intervening centuries mestizo cooking slowly evolved once stew pots began co-mingling Spanish meat and produce with native corn, chiles, herbs and other vegetables.

Corn is central to Mexican cuisine. It is the sole ingredient of *tortillas,* the ancient daily bread that has nourished generations of Mexicans. Home-made or commercially prepared dough (*masa*) made with lime-treated corn (*nixtamal*) is used to make them. If the corn for *tortillas* is lime-treated at home, it is ground on a saddle-shaped grindstone (*metate*) or taken to a mill to be ground. Patting balls of soft dough back and forth between the hands to make these round, flat cakes is a kitchen chore performed several times a day throughout the country. In the wheat-growing northern states of Mexico, *tortillas* are made of flour, and lard is added to make a flexible dough. While a *tortilla* press (a Spanish invention) makes the process easier, many urbanites no longer make their own *tortillas,* preferring to buy fresh, ready-made ones from a neighborhood *tortillería.*

17

The versatile *tortilla* is the basis of countless dishes, including appetizers and casseroles. The Spanish called foods made with *tortillas* or corn dough (*masa*) "little whims," or *antojitos*, because of their endless ingenious variety. Foods prepared from *masa* are eaten as snacks, appetizers or as a meal. Among them is the *sope* made from a thick, cooked *tortilla* pinched up around the edge to form a rim to contain a savory topping, then baked on a griddle (*comal*) when filled. This round or oval appetizer has many regional names and toppings. A round one can be a *picada, garnacha, bocol, migada* or *pellizcada*. An oval one, formed by flattening a cylinder rather than a ball of dough, can be a *memela* or *chalupa*. A *gordita* is a round or oval appetizer of fried, usually stuffed *masa* covered with toppings. Typical stuffings are refried beans and *chicharrón,* or fried pork rind. This appetizer can be made several ways. The dough can be fried first and then split to form a cavity for the filling. Some *gorditas* puff up during frying, creating a pocket for fillings. Alternatively, a depression in an uncooked dough ball can be stuffed with filling and then closed by pinching the dough together. It is then fried in oil. Crunchy, fried *tortillas* garnished with any of several toppings are *tostadas*. Pieces of *tortillas* fried to a crisp and used as a garnish or edible tableware are *totopos*.

The *tortilla* also becomes a *taco, flauta, quesadilla* and *enchilada*. A *taco* is a *tortilla* rolled around a filling, and is more typically soft (unfried) than crisp (fried). Mexican *tacos* bear no resemblance to the hard, U-shaped shells encountered north of the border. A *flauta* is a large *tortilla* rolled tightly

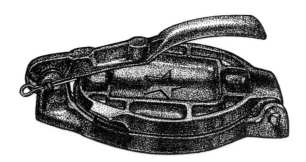

Cast-iron *tortilla* press. Available also in aluminum and wood, this inexpensive device minimizes the drudgery of patting *tortillas* out by hand and makes *tortillas* of uniform thickness. It takes much practice to accomplish this by hand.

18

around a filling to form a flutelike cylinder that is then fried until crisp. An uncooked *tortilla* folded in half over a filling and griddle-cooked becomes a *quesadilla*. The glamorous *enchilada* is a *tortilla* dipped in chile sauce then fried and wrapped around a variety of ingredients. One of the dishes most missed by Mexicans when they are out of the country for any length of time is *chilaquiles,* a casserole made with yesterday's *tortillas.*

Another ancient corn-based food is the *tamal* (singular of *tamales*) made of *masa* blended with lard until light, and steamed in corn husks, banana leaves or corn leaves. Pre-Hispanic *tamales,* however, were made without lard because animal fat was not readily available. *Tamales* often are made from the large-kerneled white corn (*cacahuazintle*) also used to make hominy. Most *tamales* are served without sauce and many contain more than just the *masa.* Typical fillings include meat, poultry, chiles, beans and squash blossoms. Sweet *tamales* have fillings of nuts, and dried and candied fruit. The dough is often tinted red with a dye made from a small insect (*cochinilla*) living on the nopal cactus. Some *tamales* have no leaf wrappers and are cooked in a casserole.

The *tamal* is also special-occasion food. It is the ritual dish for The Day of the Dead (All Saints' and All Souls' Day) fiesta on November 1st and 2nd, when the souls of the dead are believed to briefly return to the earth. At this time elaborate altars are erected at gravesites or in homes. The departed are given offerings of *tamales* and other special foods such as the "bread of the dead" (*pan de muerto*), along with favorites that were especially enjoyed during life. That *tamales* are the traditional food associated with this holiday may be attributable to the fact that the Spanish conquistadors' observation of All Souls' Day coincided with the Maya celebration of *tamales* as a special offering from the gods.

Vegetables grow almost year-round in those areas of Mexico that have mild winters. Green vegetables are more often savored in main dishes, stews, soups, vegetable puddings and fritters than eaten plain. Protein-rich beans come plain and variegated in a wide spectrum of colors, and many regional types exist. For most people, beans are are eaten three times a day and are the primary protein source. The classic dish of pot beans (*frijoles de la olla*) is a preparation of soupy boiled beans, soft but still whole. Equally popular is refried (meaning well-fried) beans (*frijoles fritos*), a dish of boiled, mashed beans fried in lard until thick and shiny. Legumes include garbanzo beans, lentils and fava beans. Flat, green seeds (*guajes*) in long tree-grown pods are eaten raw or pulverized to make a sauce called *guasmole.*

Squash is the third component of the important vegetable triad (along with corn and beans) that not only nourished Mesoamericans but feeds Mexicans today. The flesh, seeds and young shoots, or runners, of squash are eaten. Male blossoms of certain varieties are enjoyed in several ways, including stuffed. The bland squash known as *chayote* is a much-used vegetable whose edible root is prized. The root system is so extensive that it needs to be cut back annually, providing the occasion for a delicious treat to be shared with family or neighbors. Popular root vegetables are sweet potatoes, which are also candied, and the crispy jicama, always eaten raw. Vendors often leave a bit of foliage attached to a jicama root. A perky leaf or two is as an indication that the root is freshly picked and still sweet. Several lesser-known vegetables include purslane, *romeritos,* an herb resembling rosemary that is used primarily in the Christmas and Lenten dish called *revoltijo,* and *huazontle,* a wild, broccoli-flavored plant related to amaranth. In addition, several edible herbs or "greens," collectively called *quelites,* are eaten cooked or raw.

Mexico's signature foodstuff is the chile. No other cuisine revolves around chiles as it does there, despite the fact that chiles are the most widely used condiment in the world. The ubiquitous chile is used to enliven Mexican dishes of all menu categories. Even candy can be laced with powdered chiles.

Chiles occur in a wide range of sizes, colors, shapes and levels of sweetness and piquancy. Their names vary from region to region, and to add to the confusion for the neophyte, a dried chile typically has a different name than its fresh counterpart. Many varieties are available only in certain regions.

Chiles fall into two basic groups: red ones primarily used dried and green ones used fresh. Dried chiles have the stronger flavor of the two. They typically are griddle-toasted to intensify their flavor, puréed after a softening soak in water and cooked with other ingredients to make a sauce. Fresh chiles typically are chopped or puréed for sauces. Larger ones, most particularly the *chile* Poblano, are stuffed or cut into thin strips (*rajas*) after they are roasted to remove their bitter skin. Chiles are also pickled in a mild brine, becoming *chiles en escabeche.* Note: chiles should be handled carefully because they contain oils that can irritate or burn the skin or eyes.

The Indians knew the merits of a piquant sauce before the Spaniards came. Like those in common use today, the ingredients for these early sauces included chiles, tomatoes, avocados, squash seeds and herbs. *Guacamole,* the popular avocado sauce with chiles and tomatoes or tomatillos is an ancient dish of Mexico. Chiles are especially versatile because they are compatible with so many different foods. No Mexican table would be complete without at least one table sauce on it, and frequently a sauce is served in the same stone mortar (*molcajete*) in which it was prepared. *Salsa* Mexicana (also called *salsa cruda* or *salsa fresca*), an uncooked sauce of chopped tomatoes, onions and chiles flavored with cilantro, and its green equivalent, *salsa verde* (or *salsa verde cruda*), which uses cooked, tart, green tomatillos in place of tomatoes are common. These table sauces are used to flavor dishes that are not already sauced. A *mole* is a rich-flavored, complex sauce made with chiles and any of several combinations of ground nuts and seeds, spices, dried fruits, dried aromatic leaves, chocolate and *masa*. There are many regional *moles* using locally grown chiles. Cooked meat typically is simmered in the sauce, making for a hearty main dish. An *adobo* is a sauce with a liquid base of vinegar. It is a somewhat sour, thick red sauce of ground chiles, onions and herbs and it often is used for seasoning or marinating meats and fish. A sauce of ground pumpkin seeds, nuts and spices is a *pipián*.

Salads as we know them are not a part of the Mexican diet. The daily intake of lettuce is in the form of shreds sprinkled on various snack foods. A popular mixture of cooked, chopped cactus paddles with tomatoes, onions and *jalapeño* chiles is called a salad (*ensalada de nopalitos),* but it is more like a relish.

Just about every type of fruit can grow somewhere in Mexico. Many fruits uncommon in the United States are available to tempt the palate. A favorite is the bumpy-surfaced *cherimoya*. The scrumptious white pulp of this tropical beauty is sweet and juicy, and tastes like vanilla custard. The light-brown

Saddle-shaped *metate* made of volcanic rock, used to grind lime-treated corn (*nixtamal*) and other foods including *cacao,* chiles and seeds, with a roller (*mano,* or *metlapil*) also of volcanic rock. Grinding stones have been in use in Mexico for several millenia.

"Bread of the dead" (*pan de muerto*), a specialty loaf placed at gravesites for The Day of the Dead celebration as an offering to the departed. It is decorated with dough "bones" radiating out from a central "knob" representing the skull. Brilliant orange marigolds decorate gravesites at this time, possibly to guide the soul's return by their heady scent.

sapodilla (*chicozapote*) has sweet yellowish-brown, granular pulp that tastes like pears. The exotic oval *mamey* has tasty orange flesh. It and the black-fleshed *zapote negro* are used to flavor ice cream. The pulp of several fruits lends itself to the preparation of *ates,* sweet pastes made with fruit pulp cooked with sugar, which are sold in slabs and enjoyed sliced, with cheese. Cactus fruits include the *tuna* of the nopal (prickly pear) cactus and *xoconostle,* the smaller and sourer fruit of a related cactus, which is used to flavor soups. Fruits are not uncommon additions to meat dishes. *Mole manchamanteles* ("tablecloth stainer") is a dish of pork or chicken in a rich red sauce of chiles, herbs and spices, with sweet potatoes, fresh pineapple and plantains. The dish is aptly named because the sauce does indeed stain fabric. Meat stuffings (*picadillos*) include dried and candied fruit.

Mexicans love meat, and pork is the hands-down favorite. The whole animal, from fried pork rind (*chicharrón*) to the innards, is consumed with gusto. *Taco* afficionados typically have a favorite organ meat. The layer of fat surrounding the organs is rendered into lard. Pork is cooked in stews and sauced dishes, and is made into several types of sausage: *chorizo, moronga,* a blood sausage, and the linkless *longaniza.*

Large cattle ranches in northern Mexico supply much of the nation's beef. Cuts for stews and soups generally require long cooking or other means of tenderizing. Thinly sliced ordinary steaks (*bistec*) from less-tender cuts are commonplace. Dried, shredded beef (*carne machaca*) becomes a filling, while ground beef is made into meatballs to be used in such dishes as *albóndigas*. Marinated and grilled meat (*carne asada*) is popular, especially in the embellished platter (*carne asada a la* Tampiqueña) created by restaurateur José Inés Loreda, originally from Tampico. He concocted a sampler plate of a large, thin, butterflied beef fillet served with *guacamole, enchiladas,* a slab of grilled, nonmelting cheese and beans.

Uncooped chickens provide tasty meat, though it is a bit on the chewy side. Poached chicken served in a sauce such as a *pipían* or hearty *mole* is a delicious traditional main dish meal. Lamb and goat are used a great deal for *birria,* a dish of chile-marinated meat, and *barbacoa,* a dish of meat wrapped in leaves of the agave (*maguey*) plant and pit-baked.

So much of Mexico borders on the sea that it is not surprising to see many types of fish and seafood in the markets. Among them are red snapper, pompano, whitefish, jackfish, striped bass, porgy, jewfish, milkfish, snook, mackerel, rockfish, dogfish, kingfish, red clams, squid, mussels, crayfish, lobster, stone crabs and shrimp. Salt cod (*bacalao*), introduced by the Spanish after the Conquest, is imported for classic dishes such as *bacalao a la* Vizcaina, a spicy fish stew with chiles, potatoes and tomatoes, which is enjoyed at Christmas time. Popular ways to fix fish and seafood are broiling and marinating raw in lime juice (*cebiche*). Shredded seafood becomes a filling in *tacos* and *tamales.* Foods with dried shrimp are enjoyed throughout the country, especially on days when meat can not be eaten for religious reasons.

Mexico has a wonderful family of cheeses. Fresh cheese (*queso fresco*) is a salty, molded melting cheese. Soft and crumbly, it is sprinkled as a topping on many dishes. An aged, somewhat drier and stronger, crumbly cheese (*queso añejo*) is non-melting and also used to garnish food. Oaxaca's stringy white cheese (*quesillo de* Oaxaca) is cooked, pulled into long, 1-inch wide strands and rolled into balls. It is a melting cheese and is a popular choice for cheese-stuffed *quesadillas* and chiles. *Queso* Chihuahua, or *queso menonita,* is a mild, light-yellow, cheddarlike melting cheese originally introduced to the cuisine by immigrant Mennonites settling in Chihuahua. *Queso asadero* is a soft and stringy, braided cheese that can be melted directly on a griddle.

Mexican egg dishes provide hearty nourishment to start the day. *Huevos divorciados* is a colorful plate of two fried eggs, served side by side, one in green sauce and the other in red sauce, often with *chilaquiles* in the middle. Scrambled eggs in tomatillo and green chile sauce (*huevos en salsa de tomate verde*) are delicious. Eggs are also featured in the dessert category. Old World nuns in Mexican convents created many awesome sweetmeats including *yemas reales,* a dessert of baked egg yolks in cinnamon-flavored syrup with raisins. This dish is said to have originated in Puebla.

Soup is the much-enjoyed first course of the main meal. A big favorite is *sopa de tortilla,* chicken broth with chunks of chicken, roasted tomatoes, pieces of stale *tortillas,* avocado and toasted, dried chiles, served over cubes of cheese. It is also called *sopa* Azteca. Also popular are garlic soup (*sopa de ajo*) and vermicelli soup (*sopa de fideos*). Mexicans have an interesting menu category called "dry soup" (*sopa seca*). This refers to rice or pasta dishes, which are not soupy when cooked, but do start out as such. A "dry soup" is served following the "wet soup" course. The most savored is Mexican-style rice (*arroz a la* Mexicana). It is important that the grains of cooked rice remain separated. To achieve this, Mexican cooks presoak the rice in water, then rinse until the water is clear. This regimen is followed by frying the rice in a little oil until golden, most likely with a little onion and garlic. The rice is then simmered in broth with puréed tomatoes. Additional flavor depends on how the dish is garnished to taste.

It is not unusual for a restaurant to serve bread rolls, the split-topped *bolillos,* in addition to the traditional *tortillas.* For sandwiches (*tortas*), the *telera* is used. This roll has a flat, oblong shape with a triple-humped surface. It typically is heaped with so many different layers of sandwich ingredients that it appears to be bursting at the seams. Sweet breads (*pan dulce*) are especially tasty with morning coffee or tea. A favorite is the *concha,* a bun topped with sugar paste cut into a fancy shell design.

Mexican dishes call for a variety of herbs and spices. Important herbs are cilantro and *epazote,* a pungent herb that is also known as wormseed, Mexican tea and goosefoot. It is used to flavor soups and cheese fillings for *quesadillas,* and most importantly, to flavor black beans. There is no substitute for it. Avocado leaves are used for their aniselike essence, as are larger leaves known as *hoja santa.* The common spices are cumin, cloves, marjoram, bay leaves, thyme, anise, allspice, cinnamon, oregano and black pepper. Sprigs of thyme and marjoram are bundled together with bay leaves in an herb bouquet (*hierbas de olor*) for seasoning sauces, stews and stocks. Sesame and pumpkin

Epazote, a fragrant, much-used herb with a somewhat bitter taste. The plant is native to Mexico.

seeds, and nuts such as almonds, peanuts and walnuts thicken and flavor sauces.

Desserts are quite varied in Mexico and are primarily a Spanish innovation. Many have a convent tradition and are particularly rich in eggs and sugar, with cinnamon and clove flavoring. Candied sweetmeats also satisfy the desire for sugar following a meal. Crystallized fruit (*fruta cubierta*) and sugary, sweet potato pastes (*camotes*) are just a few of the candied offerings. Custard desserts include *jericalla,* a baked custard treat, *natilla,* a thin creamy custard, *cocada,* a pudding- or custard-like coconut dessert and the familar *flan.* Fruits, ice cream and ices, and gelatins are also popular. Cakes are uncommon desserts. A cake bread (*marquesote*) is sprinkled with confectioner's sugar or transformed into an *ante* by soaking it with syrup that is sometimes laced with liqueur. The cake bread is often cut in half horizontally before soaking, and filled and topped with fruit cream.

There is no reason to be thirsty in Mexico with the wonderful selection of hot and cold beverages available. The pre-Conquest hot beverage or gruel (*atole*) made of *masa* mixed with water and sweetened with unrefined sugar is still enjoyed today. Many flavorings can be used, including nuts, fruits, or chocolate. *Atole* flavored with chocolate is called *champurrado.* Traditionally, *tamales* accompany *atole.* Water-based drinks made with fruit pulp (*aguas frescas*) and water- or milk-based drinks made with fruit pulp puréed in a blender (*licuados*) are enjoyed. Some especially popular water-based drinks are *agua de jamaica,* a vivid, deep-red drink made with the dried sepals of hibiscus blossoms, and *agua de horchata,* a chalky drink made of either almonds and rice flavored with cinnamon, or ground melon seeds. Hot chocolate is a real favorite and everyone loves to eat *churros* with it. These are fluted, foot-long pieces of fried dough coated with sugar.

Throughout the countryside one will discover many unfamiliar beverages. One of them is *tejate* (*texate*), which is made of *masa,* ground *cacao* beans and *mamey* seeds, grated coconut, granulated sugar, water and a flower called *rosita de cacao*. Traditionally it is drunk out of a small, colorfully painted bowl made from a gourd.

The Spanish brought distillation techniques to the New World and before long the sugar-rich juice of the agave (*maguey*) plant was made into a liquor called *mezcal*. *Tequila* is a regional variety of *mezcal* distilled from the juice of the "blue agave." *Sangrita,* made with chile sauce and tomato, orange and lime juice, is the typical chaser. A hot fruit punch (*ponche*), usually laced with spirits, is a warming drink at Christmas time. It typically is made with guavas and *tejocotes,* small, yellow-orange fruits similar to crab apples. *Rompope* is an eggnoglike drink of convent origin, made out of alcohol, egg yolks, sugar, milk, cinnamon and vanilla. Other Mexican spirits include several fine beers and wines.

Mexico is a land of diverse regional geography. Most of it lies above 3,000 feet and not much is flat. Several mountain ranges fragment the country into numerous valleys, each with its own environment, and temperature extremes can be encountered as one travels from a tropical, coastal lowland to temperate, highland plateaus a short distance away. Because of these dramatic topological and climatic differences, the plant life and foodstuffs of each area vary considerably and regional differences in the cuisine reflect

Mezcal, a liquor distilled from the juice of the agave (*maguey*) plant. Shown here is some made in the village of Chichicapa, Oaxaca, by Del Maguey, Ltd. Co., Single Village Mezcal,™ packaged in woven, palm fiber baskets. Little ceramic cups (*copitas*) are used to drink it.

this. To illustrate the different regional culinary traditions within Mexico, we have chosen to subdivide the country into six geographic sectors as outlined in Rick Bayless's *Authentic Mexican: Regional Cooking from the Heart of Mexico*.

Northern Mexico

Northern Mexico, "El Norte," includes the states of Sonora, Chihuahua, Coahuila, Nuevo León, Tamaulipas, Baja California (Norte and Sur), Sinaloa, Durango, and the northern half of the states of Zacatecas and San Luis Potosí. Six of these have a common border with the United States. The vast, sparsely settled north encompasses an immense, semi-arid highland plateau, mountains, and flat coastal stretches, interspersed with industrial cities, including Monterrey, the third largest city in Mexico, in the state of Nuevo León. Two formidable, north-south mountain ranges, the Sierra Madre Occidental in the west, and the Sierra Madre Oriental in the east, hem in the semi-arid grass-covered plateau that supports large numbers of cattle and sheep, and goats in the more inhospitable, desertlike regions. Old World livestock, especially cattle, fared extremely well in the plains of the Mexican northland and, not surprisingly, the presence of large cattle ranches with huge herds ensured that beef was king here.

Steaks in the north tend to be huge, thick and tender, unlike the thin, quickly fried and chewy steaks more typical of the rest of Mexico. They are grilled over charcoal or wood to taste. Before refrigeration, it was necessary to dry meat to prevent spoilage and beef jerky became one of the area's typical foods. It is still featured in several regional dishes. A type of jerky (*cecina*) is made from a lengthy, continuous strip of beef that is skillfully cut from a thick slab, then salted and hung to dry. Shredded jerky (*carne machaca*) is a traditional *tortilla* filling for the popular *burrito de machaca*. Jerky is also in a scrambled egg dish (*machaca con huevo*) with tomatoes and chiles. A specialty of Chihuahua is *móchomos,* an appetizer of dried, finely shredded beef, fried until crisp. *Guacamole* is its typical accompaniment.

Goat is really big in Monterrey. Favorites are *agujas de Monterrey,* a dish of charcoal-barbecued goat short ribs, and *cabrito al pastor,* kid roasted on a stake or spit. *Cabrito en chile ancho,* or kid in *ancho* chile sauce, is a regional specialty of Zacatecas. A popular pork dish is *chilorio,* shredded pork seasoned with ground chiles and spices. This classic dish of Sinaloa often is a *taco* filling. *Caldillo de puerco,* pork stewed in chile and tomatillo sauce, will be found in Durango. A popular northern soup is *menudo estílo* Sonora, a hearty coriander-flavored beef tripe and trotter dish with hominy. Also called *menudo blanco,* it is especially popular in Sonora.

Dairy products feature prominently in northern menus. *Queso fundido con rajas y chorizo* is a northern specialty of melted, stringy cheese topped with *chorizo* and toasted, skinned strips of chiles (*rajas*), usually served in small earthenware bowls.

Spanish wheat prospered in the north, so here pale wheat flour *tortillas* (*burritos* or *burras*) are more commonplace than the corn *tortillas* ubiquitous elsewhere in Mexico, and the number one filling for them is beans. A rather curious specialty *tortilla* is the *tortilla de agua,* which is huge—up to 2 feet in diameter—and eaten like bread. This specialty of Hermosilla, Sonora, is also called *tortilla de sobaco,* or armpit, because the elastic dough used to make it extends to the armpit as it is slapped back and forth between the hands. Corn *tortillas* appear in many ways in Mexico's frontier, including *enchiladas norteñas,* a dish of stacked, unrolled corn *tortillas* with cheese and chile sauce between layers. A layered casserole of corn *tortillas* folded in half to enclose some chile, tomato and cheese sauce is *enchiladas de San Luis* or *enchiladas* Potosinas. The *masa* for this specialty of San Luis Potosí contains ground chiles.

The people of Sonora, Sinaloa, Tamaulipas and Baja California can look to the sea to enrich their diet. *Huachinango a la naranja,* or red snapper in orange sauce, is a regional dish of Sinaloa. *Callo de hacha con aguacate,* or avocado stuffed with small clams, is a specialty of Baja California Norte. In Tamaulipas, *adobo de pescado* is enjoyed. It is a dish of fish marinated in a vinegary chile sauce with onions and herbs.

Besides wheat, Mexico's northland produces tomatoes, potatoes, garbanzo beans, soybeans, chiles, corn, olives, sweet peppers, cotton, beans, avocados, pecans, walnuts, pine nuts, sugar cane and rice. Also grown are tropical and temperate fruits, and grapes for wine and brandy.

West-Central Mexico

West-Central Mexico includes the states of Nayarit, Jalisco, Guanajuato, Michoacán, Colima, Aguascalientes, Querétaro and the southern half of Zacatecas and San Luis Potosí. It encompasses the southern portion of the highland plateau between the massive coastal Sierra Madre Occidental and Oriental mountain ranges. It also includes the western end of the Sierra Madre del Sur mountain range paralleling the Pacific coast and the fertile coastal plains area of the four states bordering on the Pacific: Nayarit, Jalisco, Colima and Michoacán.

Crops produced in this region include sugar cane, wheat, rice, beans, coffee, avocados, corn, carrots, cucumbers, jicama, sesame seeds, potatoes and sweet potatoes. In Jalisco and certain areas of Guanajuato, Michoacán and Nayarit, the "blue agave" is grown for the production of *tequila*. Also produced are peaches, grapes, coconuts, strawberries, bananas, papayas, apricots, quinces, melons, guavas, citrus fruits, sapodillas (*chicozapotes*), *zapotes negros* and mangoes.

Guadalajara, the capital of Jalisco, is Mexico's second largest city. It is the home of *birria,* a dish of lamb or goat marinated in a seasoned, vinegary sauce (*adobo*) of *guajillo* and *ancho* chiles and traditionally slow-cooked in a pit oven lined with agave (*maguey*) leaves. Another specialty of Guadalajara is *mole Tapatío,* a dish of meat in *ancho* and *pasilla* chile sauce with peanuts, seasoned with cloves and cinnamon. *Torta ahogado* is a sandwich made with a sliced *bolillo* spread with refried beans, filled with barbecued pork and then dunked in a sauce of pure *arbol* chiles. It is topped with onions marinated in lime. *Pozole* is a specialty of Nayarit, Jalisco and Aguascalientes, and Guerrero in Southern Mexico. It is a hearty main-dish soup of pork and hominy. Jalisco is especially noted for its *pozole estílo* Jalisco, which has pork head and trotters in it. There are white, green and red versions of *pozole. Pozole blanco,* or white *pozole,* is made with clear broth. *Pozole verde,* or green *pozole,* gets its color from ground pumpkin seeds, tomatillos, green chiles and herbs. *Pozole rojo,* or red *pozole,* gets its color from dried red chiles. Jalisco is also home of the *flauta.*

A *cazuela,* the traditional two-handled ceramic cooking pot with glazing only on the inner surface. Attractive displays of hanging pots are in the markets.

A regional dish of Guanajuato is *enchiladas mineras* (miners'*enchiladas*) consisting of roast chicken, carrots and potatoes atop an unfolded *enchilada*. It presumably was enjoyed by silver miners in the heydey of the city of Guanajuato when it was the wealthiest mining town in the country. Some specialties of Nayarit are *camarones en frio,* or pickled shrimp, and *pollo al estílo* Ixtlan del Rio, a dish of fried chicken and potatoes topped with oregano-seasoned tomato sauce, served with chopped lettuce and zucchini in vinaigrette. It is a specialty of the city of Ixtlan del Rio.

Michoacán's unique dishes include *churipo,* beef stew with potatoes, *chayote* and rounds of corn on the cob in a *guajillo* chile sauce flavored with *epazote* and the sour cactus fruit called *xoconostle.* Plain *corundas,* irregular polyhedron-shaped *tamales* wrapped in green corn leaves, accompany the dish as bread. These *tamales* typically are served with sauces or with cream and crumbled *queso de* Cotija, a cheese made in Cotija, Michoacán. When served with *churipo,* however, the *tamales* are plain. Lake Pátzcuaro in Michoacán is famous for its whitefish. In the dish *pescado blanco de* Pátzcuaro the fish are dredged in flour, dipped in beaten eggs and fried.

Colima's noted dishes include *róbalo al perejil con langostinos,* or snook with parsley and crayfish, and *tatemado de Colima,* baked pork. Querétaro features *guichepos,* small cinnamon-flavored *tamales* made with sweetened fresh corn and milk. Popular in Aguascalientes are *pacholas,* oval ground-meat patties that have been flattened on a *metate,* fried and served with chile sauce. This state is also known for *pollo del jardin de* San Marcos, a dish of fried chicken and potatoes in chile and tomato sauce, served with fried *chorizo.* It is a traditional dish sold by vendors in the garden of St. Marcos in the city of Aguascalientes.

Sweets from the region are a specialty of Celaya, Guanajuato, called *cajeta de* Celaya, which is a thick dessert cream made of caramelized goat's milk and sugar, and small cookies from Nayarit, *gorditas de maíz horneadas,* made with corn, eggs and unrefined sugar.

Central Mexico

Central Mexico includes the states of Hidalgo, Tlaxcala, México, Morelos and Puebla. It encompasses uplands at the region where the Sierra Madre Occidental and Oriental mountain ranges coalesce with the east-west Cordillera Neovolcánica. The Valley of Mexico is one of several natural basins in this area, and Mexico City, with a population of at least 20 million, sprawls across its 2500 square miles.

Foodstuffs grown in this area include corn, rice, sugar cane, barley, tomatoes, coffee, alfalfa, wheat, beans, potatoes, avocados and peas. Apples, pears, peaches, plums, nuts, citrus fruits and mangoes are also grown here.

One of the most famous dishes of Central Mexico is *barbacoa,* or barbecued lamb or kid traditionally wrapped in *maguey* leaves and slow-cooked in a pit. This Sunday special is served with *salsa borracha,* a hot chile sauce containing *pulque.* In Tlaxcala a favorite way to eat barbecued lamb is *barbacoa en mixiote.* Lamb in chile sauce with anise-flavored avocado leaves is steamed in a piece of parchmentlike skin (*mixiote*) from a *maguey* leaf.

A specialty of Mexico City is *Budín Azteca,* a many-layered casserole of *tortillas,* shredded chicken, cheese and strips of toasted, skinned chiles, with tomatillo sauce. Another specialty of Mexico City is *caldo* Tlalpeño, a smoky, *epazote*-flavored chicken broth with shredded chicken, vegetables, *chipotle* chiles and rice, garnished with avocado. The dish originated in Tlalpán, once a rural village, but now a part of Mexico City. Corn fungus (*cuitlacoche*) is considered a delicacy in Mexico City and it appears in several types of dishes including patés, crêpes and soups such as the popular *sopa de cuitlacoche.*

There are many delicious specialties of Mexico State. *Pancita de carnero rellana,* a preparation of mutton tripe filled with offal and pit-barbecued with

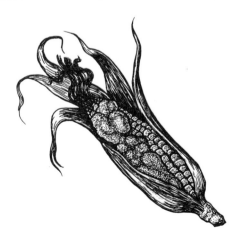

An ear of corn deformed by the fungus called *cuitlacoche* growing as a gray-black mass inside the kernels. This fungus has been eaten since pre-Columbian times. Drawn from *Rick Bayless's Mexican Kitchen* by Rick Bayless.

meat, then served sliced, is found in San Juan Teotihuacán and Texcoco, Mexico State. A local favorite in Toluca, the capital of Mexico State, is the *huarache,* an oval, foot-long *tortilla* made of coarsely ground white or blue corn. It can be munched on plain or topped with sauce, chile slices and fine cheese threads. It is also the name of a large, fried oval of *masa* topped with red sauce on one side, green sauce on the other, all buried under chopped onions and shredded cheese. This *huarache* is a marketplace item in Mexico City. Toluca is famous for sausage, and its *chorizo verde* made with pork is a real winner. Served many ways, it is delicious and bright green, thanks to a goodly amount of tomatillos, green chiles and cilantro.

Puebla's convent kitchens produced several of Mexico's outstanding classic dishes. One of the most significant is *chiles en nogada.* This is a spectacular, patriotic-looking dish of Poblano chiles stuffed with a seasoned meat and candied fruit mixture, topped with fresh walnut sauce and garnished with pomegranate seeds. Considered Mexico's national dish—red, white and green like the flag—it is available in late summer when fresh nuts are available. The dish is said to have originated to honor Don Agustín de Iturbide, who negotiated a compromise in 1821 to end the Independence War between Mexico and Spain. Another classic is *mole* Poblano *de guajolote,* a dish of turkey with a dark, complex sauce of *mulato, ancho, pasilla* and *chipotle* chiles, dried fruits, nuts, spices and chocolate. Puebla is also justly famous for its *tinga* Poblana, a stew of shredded pork in tomato and *chipotle* chile sauce, and *camotes de* Santa Clara, sugary pastes made of sweet potatoes rolled like cigars and wrapped in paper.

The *chile* Poblano (right), a large, fresh chile that when dried is called the *chile ancho* (left). The fresh chile is a key ingredient in Mexico's national dish, *chiles en nogada,* created in Puebla.

Tlaxcala's specialties include two tasty drinks. *Atole de alegría* is a warm drink made of toasted amaranth seeds and unrefined sugar, flavored with cinnamon. *Chileatole* is a drink made of fermented corn with chiles. It is also an *epazote*-flavored soup made with ground *masa,* fresh corn kernels and chiles. Regional dishes of Hidalgo are *ximbo,* a preparation of fish cooked in *maguey* leaves, and *asado al pastor,* whole mutton grilled on a stake over fire. It is served with *salsa borracha.* In Morelos, *clemole* is a specialty meat and vegetable stew in chile sauce. Also typical is *migas de* Morelos, an oregano-flavored soupy dish of bread, eggs, *longaniza,* chiles and cheese.

Gulf Coastal Mexico

Gulf Coastal Mexico includes the state of Veracruz and the western half of Tabasco. This region contains the hot coastal lowlands and steamy jungle along the Gulf of Mexico. Produce grown in this area includes beans, rice, allspice, sweet potatoes, *cacao,* sugar cane, coffee and vanilla beans. Other crops are coconuts, *mamey,* bananas, mangoes, tamarinds, oranges, guavas, papayas, grapefruits, pineapples, tangerines and the cashew apple (*marañón*).

One of Veracruz' most famous dishes is *hauchinango a la* Veracruzana, a preparation of red snapper (*hauchinango*) baked in a seasoned sauce of tomatoes, chiles, green olives and plump capers. *Chilpachole de jaiba* is also a specialty. This is a spicy soup made with small blue crabs (*jaibas*) and *chipotle* chiles. *Arroz a la tumbada* is a seafood and rice dish reminiscent of Spain's *paella,* with *jalapeño* chiles and tomatoes. *Caldo largo de* Alvarado is a fish and seafood soup specialty of the port city of Alvarado. Also typical is *tamales estilo* Veracruzano, *tamales* steamed in banana leaves and an anise-flavored, heart-shaped leaf called *hoja santa.*

The rivers of Tabasco provide plenty of fish, including the popular garfish (*pejelagarto*). This fish is often enjoyed smoked, and a typical way to prepare it is in the scrambled eggs dish called *huevos con pejelagarto.* Crayfish (*piguas*) are also a prized catch from the river and are enjoyed stuffed with garlic (*piguas al ajo*). Other regional specialties are *tamalito de chipilín,* a *tamal* made with *masa* mixed with the aromatic herb called *chipilín,* and *pozol,* a water-based drink made with *masa,* or corn dough, mixed with ground *cacao* beans and sweetened with sugar. It traditionally is drunk out of cups made of gourds.

Red snapper (*huachinango*), a much-esteemed fish in Mexico, showcased whole or cut into fillets in Veracruz-style red snapper, or *huachinango a la* Veracruzana.

Southern Mexico

Southern Mexico includes the states of Guerrero, Oaxaca and Chiapas. This region encompasses rugged uplands with many valleys, including the Valley of Oaxaca, formed by a convergence of three river valleys. Along the Pacific coast are the Sierra Madre del Sul mountains in Guerrero and Oaxaca, and the Sierra Madre de Chiapas in Chiapas. Lowlands comprise the Pacific coastal plains and the Isthmus of Tehuantepec, the narrow constriction between the ancient land of the Maya in the Yucatán and the rest of Mexico.

Crops grown are sugar cane, corn, coffee, tomatoes, zucchini, rice, sesame seeds, *cacao,* peanuts, anise seeds, annatto seeds, *chilacayotes* (a local pumpkin), papayas, chiles, onions, carrots, radishes and agave for *mezcal.* Also produced are melons, *cherimoyas,* bananas, guavas, oranges, limes, pomegranates, mangoes and tamarind.

Regional specialties of Guerrero include *pozole,* the pork and hominy stew, *taquitos,* a preparation of *tacos* rolled around *requesón,* a cheese similar to cottage cheese, and *codorniz a la talla,* grilled, butterflied quail served in spicy tomato and chile sauce. Also typical is *filetes de mojarra en totomoxtle,* fillets of a small, silvery fish steamed in corn husks with chopped nopal cactus paddles.

Oaxaca is the land of the *mole.* There are a great many Oaxacan *moles* but the seven most famous come to mind first: *amarillo, chichilo, coloradito, colorado, negro, rojo* and *verde* (see *Foods & Flavors Guide* for an individual sauce's many ingredients). Cooked meats typically are simmered in *moles* to make a rich main meal. Not a one should be missed. *Caldo de camarón* is shrimp broth made here with dried shrimp. A well-liked street snack is *tortilla con asiento* made with a *blanda,* a thin, soft, white-corn *tortilla* topped with *asiento,* a Oaxacan kitchen staple of well-cooked pork fat and crumbs of fried pork skin. Another local street food is the hard, foot-wide specialty *tortilla* called a *tlayuda,* covered with *asiento,* refried beans, string cheese and several other choices of toppings, including strips of *chile de agua,* the local chile. *Cecina enchilada,* thinly sliced pork in a vinegary chile marinade, is Oaxaca's version of the North's beef *cecina. Abulón al mojo de ajo,* abalone in browned garlic sauce, is local to the Isthmus of Tehuantepec.

Chiapas is known for a dried specialty sausage called *butifarra,* which is colored red with *achiote* and flavored with allspice. Black beans are popular in southern Mexico, and in Chiapas they typically are flavored with the aromatic herb *chipilín* to make *frijoles con chipilín.* A popular dish in the city of Tuxtla Gutiérrez is *carne cocida en limón,* a preparation of seasoned raw, ground meat marinated in lime juice. *Sopa de pan,* bread soup with vegetables, is a specialty of San Cristóbal de las Casas.

The Yucatán

The Yucatán is comprised of the states of Yucatán, Quintana Roo, Campeche and the eastern half of Tabasco. Much of the land is flat and underlaid by limestone. Rivers are uncommon. In the dry northern part of the Yucatán, water can be obtained from large subterranean sinkholes (*cenotes*). Some of the produce of this area is rice, sugar cane, *habanero* and *xcat-ik* chiles, *achiote* (annatto), cucumbers, *chaya* (a local chardlike vegetable), chayote, manioc, coconuts, red onions, sapodillas (*chicozapotes*) and *mamey.*

Seasoning pastes called *recados* are used in many Yucatecan dishes. *Achiote,* a much-used spice in this region, provides a nutty flavor and a brick-red color to dishes, and it is a key ingredient of *recado rojo.* A classic dish of Yucatán is *cochinita pibil*, pork covered with *recado rojo,* wrapped in banana leaves and slow-cooked in a pit (*pib*). Banana leaves are the important food wrappers in this part of Mexico.

Pickling foods in marinades is characteristic of the area. *Cebollas en escabeche,* pickled red onions, is a popular relish or garnish. A popular pickled dish in Tabasco is *ostiones en escabeche,* or pickled oysters.

Papadzules, tortillas dipped in a pumpkin seed sauce and filled with crumbled hard-boiled eggs is a famous old dish of the Yucatán. It is garnished with tomato sauce and decorated with green oil squeezed from the seeds. A popular *masa* snack is *panuchos estílo* Yucatán, a fried *tortilla* that puffs during cooking to form a pocket, which is stuffed with fried black beans and hard-boiled egg slices. It is garnished with pickled shredded meat and pickled purple onions. Mérida, capital of Yucatán, is rightly proud of its *sopa de lima,* a soup with vegetables, shredded chicken, pieces of the local bitter lime (*lima agria*) and fried *tortilla* pieces, all garnished to taste with chopped *serrano* chiles.

Specialties of Quintana Roo are *cerdo con frijoles, epazote*-flavored pork and black beans cooked with chiles, and *cherna al* Quintana Roo, jewfish fillets marinated in lime and simmered in a vinegary tomato and chile sauce seasoned with cumin and oregano. In Campeche, *cazón* (dogfish, or shark) is abundant and a local preparation is *cazón a la* Campechana made with fillets fried with tomatoes and *habanero* chiles, flavored with *epazote.*

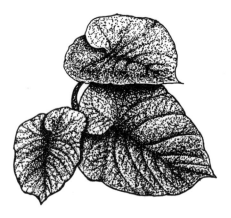

Hoja santa, soft, heart-shaped, green leaves with an anise-like flavor. They are used fresh as a wrapper for *tamales* or fish, and to season sauces, predominantly in the Gulf Coastal and Southern Mexico regions.

Tastes of Mexico

You are encouraged to try some of our favorite Mexican recipes before you leave home. This is a wonderful and immediately rewarding way to preview the extraordinary cuisine of Mexico. Most of the special Mexican ingredients necessary for these recipes are available in the United States (see *Resources,* p. 61). Satisfactory substitutes are given for unavailable ones. Please see our *Notes for Working with Chiles* on p. 58 for tips that will be helpful in preparing many Mexican dishes.

APPETIZERS/SNACKS

Cebiche de Jicama

Jicama seviche. Serves 4–6.

This recipe was provided by Timothy Mello, a chef in Nogales-Santa Cruz County, Arizona. He heads the Tourism & Travel Development committee for the Chamber of Commerce to spotlight cultural heritage initiatives and culinary destinations in Arizona and Mexico. *Cebiche de jicama* is a *botana,* or snack, to accompany *tequila* or ice-cold beer.

> 4½ POUNDS JICAMA, PEELED, WASHED AND GRATED OR
>
>   FINELY DICED
>
> 6 SCALLIONS, CHOPPED
>
> 8 *SERRANO* CHILES,* FINELY DICED
>
> JUICE OF 1 POUND OF LIMES (4 OR 5)
>
> SALT TO TASTE
>
> 1 BUNCH CILANTRO, COARSELY CHOPPED
>
> 1 POUND VERY RIPE TOMATOES, DICED (SEEDED, OPTIONAL)

In a large bowl combine jicama, scallions and chiles with lime juice and salt to taste. After a few minutes, add cilantro and tomato. Gently mix together. Serve immediately with *tostaditas* or *totopos* (pieces of fried *tortilla* chips).

*Available at markets carrying Hispanic foods; also see *Resources* (p. 61) for online suppliers of Mexican foods.

Flor de Calabaza Relleno de Requesón

Squash flowers stuffed with farmer's cheese. Serves 12.

The recipe for this appetizer was provided by Susana Trilling, teacher, chef and restaurateur, who lives in the foothills of Oaxaca and runs the popular cooking school, Seasons of My Heart. This glamorous dish is perfect for a fancy meal.

24 SQUASH FLOWERS

Vegetable filling

1 WHOLE EAR OF CORN

1 SPRIG *EPAZOTE,** OPTIONAL

3 TABLESPOONS OLIVE OR SUNFLOWER OIL

½ MEDIUM WHITE ONION, FINELY CHOPPED

½ POUND ZUCCHINI, FINELY CHOPPED

⅛ POUND MUSHROOMS, FINELY CHOPPED

7 CLOVES GARLIC, FINELY CHOPPED

¼ CUP PUMPKIN SEEDS (ABOUT 1 OUNCE), HULLED

3 PEPPERCORNS

1 ALLSPICE BERRY

1 TABLESPOON *JALAPEÑO* CHILE JUICE,* FROM PICKLED *JALAPEÑOS*

10 *EPAZOTE* LEAVES,* OR SUBSTITUTE 4 STEMS CILANTRO

½ TEASPOON SALT

Cheese filling

½ POUND *REQUESÓN,** OR SUBSTITUTE FARMER'S CHEESE OR FRESH RICOTTA

¼ TEASPOON CINNAMON PIECES, TOASTED AND GROUND

2 EGGS

¼ TEASPOON GROUND BLACK PEPPER

1 TABLESPOON CILANTRO LEAVES, FINELY CHOPPED

1 TABLESPOON *CHEPIL* LEAVES,* OR SUBSTITUTE CILANTRO

SALT TO TASTE

Tomato broth

2 POUNDS RIPE TOMATOES

2 BIG *PASILLA DE* OAXACA CHILES, STEMMED, SEEDED
    AND DEVEINED, OR SUBSTITUTE *CHIPOTLE* CHILES

2 TABLESPOONS SUNFLOWER OIL

½ MEDIUM WHITE ONION, FINELY CHOPPED

7 CLOVES GARLIC, FINELY CHOPPED

Dredging and frying

½ CUP UNBLEACHED FLOUR

½ TEASPOON SALT

½ TEASPOON PEPPER

½ CUP SUNFLOWER OIL

Degrain corn cob, reserving kernels. Put cob of corn, *epazote* and 2 cups of water in small saucepan and bring to a boil. Cover and simmer for at least ½ hour to make "corn stock." Strain and reserve stock.

Wash and clean squash flowers, removing stamens inside and sepals from the outside, keeping flowers and stems intact. Soak flowers in a bowl of water for 5 minutes, then dry carefully with a dish towel.

To make vegetable filling, heat oil in medium saucepan over medium heat. Sauté onions until clear, about 3 minutes. Add squash and corn, and sauté 10 minutes longer. Add mushrooms and garlic, and sauté 5 minutes longer.

In a small, dry frying pan, toast pumpkin seeds over medium heat, stirring, until they puff up and have a nutty brown color. Remove from pan and cool. Add peppercorns and allspice to pan, and toast until they give off their scent, about 2 minutes. Grind with pumpkin seeds in a *molcajete* or blender to a medium grind, not a powder. Add seed mixture to vegetables, stirring well. Add *jalapeño* pickling juice and one cup corn stock to vegetable mixture. Cover and simmer for 20 minutes. Add salt to taste. Turn off heat and add *epazote* or cilantro leaves.

To make the cheese filling, whip cheese, cinnamon, eggs, black pepper, cilantro leaves and *chepil* for about 5 minutes with a whisk or fork. Add salt to taste.

To make the tomato sauce, add tomatoes to one quart of boiling water in a medium saucepan, and boil 3 minutes. Remove tomatoes and set aside to cool. In a heated dry *comal* or frying pan, toast chiles on both sides until they blister and give off their scent. Place chiles in hot tomato water to soften for 10 minutes. Remove skin and blend chiles with tomatoes in a blender until smooth. Heat 2 tablespoons oil in a heavy frying pan. Sauté onions until clear, about 3 minutes. Add garlic and sauté for 1 minute more. Add tomato and chile mixture. Cover and simmer for 20 minutes. Add salt and pepper to taste.

To stuff squash flowers, carefully open each flower and put in one tablespoon vegetable mixture. Top with one tablespoon cheese mixture and enclose with petals. Heat sunflower oil in large frying pan over medium heat. Dredge stuffed flowers through flour, shaking off excess. Make sure petals still enclose stuffing. Fry flowers in oil, 3 or 4 at a time, turning once, until golden brown. Drain on paper towels.

To serve, ladle ¼ cup of the tomato sauce on each plate and place two flowers on top. Garnish with squash leaves or parsley.

*Available at markets carrying Hispanic foods; also see *Resources* (p. 61) for online suppliers of Mexican foods.

SOUPS

Sopa Tarasca

Tarascan soup. Serves 8.

This recipe was reprinted by permission of John Wiley & Sons, Inc., from *Hidden Cuisines of Mexico* by Bruce Kraig and Dudley Nieto; copyright © 1996 by Bruce Kraig and Dudley Nieto. It was created by Sr. Felipe Oseguera Iturbide, Pátzcuaro, Michoacán. Bruce Kraig, PhD, Professor of History at Roosevelt University, Chicago, teaches courses in culinary history and ancient civilizations, and has written and hosted two programs for public television on Mexican food and culture.

> 6 WHOLE *ANCHO* CHILES,* STEMMED, SEEDED AND DEVEINED
>
> 6 TABLESPOONS CANOLA OIL
>
> 1 MEDIUM ONION, FINELY CHOPPED
>
> 2 CLOVES GARLIC, FINELY CHOPPED
>
> 1 CUP TOMATO PURÈE
>
> 8½ CUPS WATER
>
> 4 WHOLE BAY LEAVES
>
> 4 SPRIGS FRESH THYME
>
> 2 SPRIGS MARJORAM
>
> 4 CUPS CHICKEN STOCK
>
> 1 TEASPOON FRESHLY GROUND PEPPER
>
> ¼ CUP OR MORE CANOLA OIL
>
> 10 WHOLE *TORTILLAS,* CUT INTO STRIPS AND DEEP FRIED
>
> 12 OUNCES *FRESCO* CHEESE, CRUMBLED*
>
> 1¼ CUP SOUR CREAM
>
> 1 AVOCADO, PEELED AND CUBED.

Cover chiles with hot water and set aside. Heat oil in a deep soup pot. Add onion and sauté until clear. Add garlic and tomato purée. Heat to simmer and cook for 3 minutes. Stir in chicken stock, herbs and black pepper. Heat to simmer and cook for 10 minutes. While soup is cooking, heat canola oil in a deep, heavy skillet. Add tortilla strips in batches and fry. Drain on paper towels. Place 1½ cups soup in bowl of a food processor or blender. Remove chiles from water and cut in julienne strips. Add ⅓ cup of the julienned *ancho* chiles and strips from one of the fried *tortillas*. Process until mixture forms a thick purée. Stir this purée into the soup and mix well. Simmer for an additional 5–10 minutes. To serve, place *tortilla* strips and sour cream in each bowl. Cover with soup. Garnish with julienned *ancho* chiles, cubed avocados and cheese.

*Available at markets carrying Hispanic foods; also see Resources (p. 61) for online suppliers of Mexican foods.

Crema de Nuez

Cream of walnut soup. Serves 12.

The recipe for this elegant soup was reprinted with permission of Council Oak
Books from *Mexico's Feasts of Life* by Patricia Quintana (see cover); copyright © 1994
by Patricia Quintana.

Broth

6 QUARTS WATER

½ STEWING CHICKEN

4 CHICKEN LEGS (DRUMSTICK AND THIGH)

½ POUND VEAL

3 WHOLE CARROTS, PEELED

1 WHOLE LEEK WITH GREEN TOP, WASHED

½ CUP CELERY, WITH LEAVES, WASHED

2 MEDIUM WHITE ONIONS, PEELED AND HALVED

½ GARLIC HEAD, CUT IN HALF ACROSS THE GRAIN

1 SMALL TURNIP, PEELED

3 BAY LEAVES

1 SPRIG FRESH (½ TEASPOON DRIED) THYME

1 SPRIG FRESH (½ TEASPOON DRIED) MARJORAM

10 WHOLE BLACK PEPPERCORNS

10 WHOLE ALLSPICE

SALT OR POWDERED BOUILLON TO TASTE

Sauce

5 TABLESPOONS BUTTER, AT ROOM TEMPERATURE

¼ CUP RICE FLOUR OR CORNSTARCH

¼ CUP ALL-PURPOSE FLOUR

½ MEDIUM WHITE ONION, PEELED AND QUARTERED

2 RIBS CELERY

½ LEEK, SLICED LENGTHWISE

3 CUPS WALNUTS OR PECANS, GROUND FINE IN SPICE MILL

　　OR FOOD PROCESSOR

2 CUPS WHIPPING CREAM

1 TEASPOON NUTMEG

SALT TO TASTE

[Crema de Nuez, *continued*]

> *Garnish*
>
> 1 CUP WALNUTS, GROUND (OPTIONAL)
>
> ½ CUP PARSLEY OR CHIVES, FINELY CHOPPED (OPTIONAL)
>
> POMEGRANATE SEEDS (OPTIONAL)

To prepare broth, heat water in a large saucepan or stockpot. Add chicken, veal, carrots, leek, celery, onion, garlic, turnip, bay leaves, thyme, marjoram, peppercorns, allspice and salt. Bring to a boil, skim, reduce to simmer and cook 1½ hours. Skim off fat. Strain and reserve broth, reserving chicken and veal for another use if desired. Or begin with previously made chicken broth.

To prepare sauce, heat butter in a large saucepan or stockpot. Stir in rice flour and all-purpose flour and cook, stirring, until flour begins to brown. Stir in chicken broth (12–14 cups) gradually with a whisk, being sure that the mixture is smooth. Wrap onion, celery and leek in cheesecloth and place in broth. Simmer for 20 minutes. Remove cheesecloth bag with vegetables. Add nuts, cream and nutmeg. Simmer an additional 20–25 minutes. If soup thickens too much, thin with broth or milk. This soup may be served from a hollowed-out pumpkin or squash. Garnish as desired.

Vegetables

Arroz Verde con Chiles Rellenos

Green rice with stuffed chiles. Serves 6.

The recipe for this popular Lenten dish in Mexico was reprinted by permission of Clarkson N. Potter, Inc., a division of Crown Publishers, Inc., from *My Mexico* by Diana Kennedy; copyright © 1998 by Diana Kennedy.

> 1¼ CUPS LONG-GRAIN WHITE RICE
>
> HOT WATER TO COVER
>
> 1 LARGE BUNCH ITALIAN PARSLEY
>
> 1 CLOVE GARLIC, PEELED
>
> ½ SMALL ONION
>
> ⅓ CUP WATER
>
> ½ CUP PEANUT OR SAFFLOWER OIL
>
> 4 CUPS MILK
>
> 2 TEASPOONS SALT, OR TO TASTE
>
> 6 SMALL *CHILES* POBLANO, ROASTED AND PEELED OR
>
> 6 LARGE CANNED, PEELED GREEN CHILES
>
> ½ TO ¾ POUND MILD CHEDDAR CHEESE

Pour hot water over rice and let it stand for about 25 minutes. Drain rice and wash it in cold water until washing water is clear. Shake colander well and leave rice to drain for a while. Wash parsley well, remove coarse stems and put leaves and sprigs into a blender with garlic, onion and water. Blend to a smooth sauce. Set aside.

Heat oil in flameproof dish. Give rice a final shake to get rid of any excess water. When oil is very hot, stir in rice, making sure that as many grains as possible get coated with oil. Cook rice over high flame, stirring it from time to time, until it becomes a pale golden color—about 10 minutes. Tip dish to one side and drain off some of excess oil. Hold back rice with back of a large metal spoon and let oil drain away from it. Stir blended parsley into rice and cook for 2 minutes more. Stir milk and salt well into rice and let mixture come to a boil. Lower flame, cover dish tightly, and let rice cook very slowly for 15 minutes (see note below).

Meanwhile prepare chiles. Cut chiles down one side and carefully remove seeds. Cut cheese into thick slices and stuff chiles well. Set chiles well into rice, slit side up to prevent stuffing from seeping out. Cover dish and continue cooking rice over low flame for another 15 minutes. Serve as a separate course, 1 chile per person with rice.

Note: Up to point of adding milk and cooking rice slowly, the dish can be prepared ahead of time.

Purée de Papas

Potato purée. Serves 6.

This recipe was reprinted, with slight changes, by permission of Macmillan USA, a Simon & Schuster Macmillan Company, from *The Food and Life of Oaxaca: Traditional Recipes from Mexico's Heart* by Zarela Martínez; copyright © 1997 by Zarela Martínez. Zarela is chef-owner of the very popular New York restaurant, Zarela. This dish from the Isthmus of Tehuantepec, Oaxaca, is one of her favorites.

6 MEDIUM-SIZE RUSSET OR OTHER STARCHY POTATOES, ABOUT 2½–3

POUNDS, SCRUBBED AND QUARTERED BUT UNPEELED

2 MEDIUM-SIZE CARROTS, PEELED AND CUT INTO ¼-INCH DICE

1 CUP TINY NEW PEAS, FRESH OR FROZEN

¾ CUP MEXICAN *CREMA,** OR HEAVY CREAM

1 LARGE EGG, BEATEN

2 TEASPOONS (OR TO TASTE) PREPARED YELLOW MUSTARD

4 TABLESPOONS (½ STICK) UNSALTED BUTTER

1 MEDIUM-SIZE ONION, FINELY CHOPPED

1 LARGE GARLIC CLOVE, MINCED

¼ CUP ITALIAN PARSLEY LEAVES, MINCED

[Purée de Papas, *continued*]

> 1 3-OUNCE JAR PICKLED PEARL ONIONS, DRAINED
>
> ½ CUP PITTED GREEN OLIVES, DRAINED AND SLICED
>
> ¼ CUP (OR TO TASTE) PICKLED *JALAPEÑO* CHILES,* DRAINED
>
>   AND FINELY CHOPPED
>
> FRESHLY GROUND BLACK PEPPER
>
> ½ TEASPOON SALT (OPTIONAL)

Prepare the vegetables. Have ready a medium-size saucepan of boiling salted water. Add potatoes and cook until tender, about 12–15 minutes. Lift out, letting them drain well, and peel. Set aside. Add diced carrots and cook until crisp-tender, about 5 minutes. Scoop out with a strainer or slotted spoon and set aside. Add peas and cook until barely tender, about 3 minutes; remove and drain.

In a large bowl, mash potatoes with a potato masher. Add *crema* and beat with a wooden spoon to eliminate most of the lumps. Add egg and mustard, continuing to beat until mixture is smooth and fluffy.

Preheat oven to 350°F. In a medium-size skillet, melt butter over medium-high heat until fragrant and sizzling but not browned. Add onion and garlic and cook, stirring, for 3 minutes, until onion is clear. Add parsley, cook for 1 minute longer, and beat mixture into mashed potatoes. Stir in diced carrots, peas, pickled onion, olives and *jalapeños*. Taste for seasoning and add the pepper and optional salt. Transfer mixture to a buttered 2-quart baking dish and bake 20 minutes. Serve at once.

*Available at markets carrying Hispanic foods; also see *Resources* (p. 61) for online suppliers of Mexican foods.

Quelites con Frijoles, Estílo Veracruzano

Veracruz-style greens and beans with red chiles and dumplings. Serves 6.

This recipe was reprinted by permission of Scribner, a Division of Simon & Schuster, from *Rick Bayless's Mexican Kitchen: Capturing the Vibrant Flavors of a World-Class Cuisine* by Rick Bayless; copyright © 1996 by Richard Lane Bayless. Rick Bayless's Mexican restaurants in Chicago, Frontera and Topolobampo, are legendary.

> 1 POUND (ABOUT 2½ CUPS) DRY BLACK BEANS
>
> 4 *CHIPOTLE* CHILES,* STEMMED (OR CANNED *CHIPOTLE*
>
>   CHILES *EN ADOBO*)
>
> 3 MEDIUM (1½ OUNCES TOTAL) DRIED *ANCHO* CHILES,*
>
>   STEMMED AND SEEDED
>
> 3 GARLIC CLOVES, PEELED AND ROUGHLY CHOPPED
>
> ½ SMALL WHITE ONION, SLICED

4 TABLESPOONS OLIVE OR VEGETABLE OIL OR RICH-TASTING LARD

1 CUP (8 OUNCES) FRESH *MASA** FOR *TORTILLAS* OR A GENEROUS

¾ CUP DRIED *MASA HARINA** MIXED WITH ⅔ CUP HOT WATER

SALT, ABOUT 2½ TEASPOONS

¾ CUP CILANTRO, CHOPPED

1½ CUPS (6 OUNCES) CRUMBLED MEXICAN *QUESO FRESCO** OR PRESSED,

   SALTED FARMER'S CHEESE

6 CUPS STURDY GREENS SUCH AS LAMB'S QUARTERS (*QUELITES*),* CHARD OR

   COLLARD, STEMMED AND THICKLY SLICED

Rinse beans, then scoop them into a large (6-quart) pot, preferably a Dutch oven or Mexican earthenware *olla*. Add 2 quarts water and remove any beans that float. Bring to a boil, reduce heat to medium-low and simmer, partially covered, until beans are tender (they will taste creamy, not chalky), about 2 hours. Stir regularly and add water to keep liquid level a generous ½ inch above beans.

On an ungreased griddle or heavy skillet over medium heat, toast dried *chipotles*, turning regularly and pressing flat with a spatula, until they are very aromatic and a little toasty smelling, about 30 seconds. (Canned *chipotles* need no preparation.) Open *anchos* flat and, 1 or 2 at a time, press flat in the skillet for a few seconds with a metal spatula until they start to crackle—even send up a faint wisp of smoke—then flip and press down to toast other side. In a small bowl, cover chiles with hot water and let rehydrate 30 minutes, stirring frequently to ensure even soaking. Drain and discard water.

In a blender, purée chiles with garlic, onion and ½ cup water (you may need a little more to get everything moving). Press through a medium-mesh strainer into a bowl. In a large saucepan, heat 2 tablespoons oil or lard over medium-high. Add purée all at once and stir nearly constantly as it sears and thickens for about 5 minutes. When beans are tender, add chile purée and simmer 30 minutes more.

In a large bowl, knead together fresh or reconstituted *masa* with remaining 2 table-spoons of oil or lard, ½ teaspoon salt, ¼ cup chopped cilantro and cheese. Form into about 48 balls. Cover and set aside.

There should be a good amount of broth in the beans (you have to add dumplings and greens and still come out with a stewlike consistency, so add water if necessary), and the broth should be as thick as a light sauce (if it's not as thick as you like, purée a cup of beans in a food processor or blender and return to pot to thicken them). Liberally season stew with salt, usually about 2 teaspoons.

With pot simmering over medium heat, add dumplings one at a time, nestling them into gurgling broth. Simmer 5 minutes, then add greens. Stir *gently* so as not to break up the dumplings and simmer until greens are fully cooked (about 7 minutes for tender greens like chard, 10–12 minutes for collard and lamb's quarters). Ladle into warm bowls, sprinkle with chopped cilantro and serve with steaming *tortillas*.

[Quelites con Frijoles, Estílo Veracruzano, *continued*]

Advance preparation: the beans can be cooked several days ahead, through the step of simmering 30 minutes in chile purée; cover and refrigerate. The dumplings can be formed a day ahead; cover them, too, and refrigerate. Reheat the beans slowly before adding the dumplings and greens.

Variations and improvisations: for a smoky taste, cook beans with a ham hock. Or, add ½ pound peeled shrimp just before adding dumplings. Or, ladle a cup of stew into a pasta bowl, then lay a grilled pork chop on top.

*Available at markets carrying Hispanic foods; also see *Resources* (p. 61) for online suppliers of Mexican foods.

VEGETABLE SALADS/RELISHES

Ensalada de Nopalitos

Prickly pear cactus paddle salad. Serves 6–8.

This recipe was reprinted by permission of William Morrow & Company, Inc., from *The El Paso Chile Company's Texas Border Cookbook* by W. Park Kerr, Norma Kerr and Michael McLaughlin; copyright © 1992 by W. Park Kerr, Norma Kerr and Michael McLaughlin. The Kerrs run the El Paso Chile Company, El Paso, Texas.

> 1 LARGE, HEAVY SWEET RED PEPPER
>
> 4½ TEASPOONS SALT
>
> 1 POUND *NOPALES*,* SPINES REMOVED, TOUGH EDGES TRIMMED,
>> CUT INTO LONG ¼-INCH STRIPS
>
> TOPS OF 4 GREEN ONIONS
>
> 6–8 PICKLED *JALAPEÑO* CHILES,* STEMMED AND CUT INTO JULIENNE
>
> 3 TABLESPOONS FRESH LIME JUICE
>
> 2 TABLESPOONS OLIVE OIL
>
> 2 JUICY, RIPE MEDIUM TOMATOES, TRIMMED AND CUT INTO WEDGES
>
> 1 BUTTERY-RIPE BLACK-SKINNED AVOCADO, PITTED AND CUT INTO
>> THIN, UNPEELED WEDGES
>
> 1 SMALL RED ONION, PEELED AND SLICED INTO THIN RINGS
>
> 4 OUNCES CRUMBLED SOFT WHITE CHEESE SUCH AS FETA OR GOAT CHEESE

In the open flame of a gas burner or under a preheated broiler, roast the red pepper, turning it, until peel is evenly charred. In a closed paper bag or in a bowl covered with a plate, steam pepper until cool. Rub away blackened skin, stem and core pepper, and cut flesh into julienne.

Over high heat, bring a medium pan of water to a boil. Stir in 2 teaspoons of salt and *nopalitos*. Cook 3 minutes, then drain and rinse *nopalitos* under cold running water. Fill pan with fresh cold water, set over medium heat and bring to a boil. Stir in 2 teaspoons of salt, *nopalitos*, and green onion tops and bring to a boil. Lower heat and simmer about 10 minutes, or until *nopalitos* are tender and no longer slippery. Drain and transfer them to a bowl of iced water. When they are cool, drain thoroughly.

In a large bowl toss together roasted red pepper, *nopalitos,* and pickled *jalapeños.* Add lime juice, olive oil, and ½ teaspoon of salt and toss again. Adjust seasoning.

Arrange *nopalito* mixture on serving plate. Top with tomato wedges, avocado wedges and red onion slices. Scatter crumbled cheese over all and serve immediately.

*Available at markets carrying Hispanic foods; also see *Resources* (p. 61) for online suppliers of Mexican foods.

MAIN DISHES

Churipo Doña Paca

Beef and vegetable stew, Doña Paca. Serves 6–8.

This recipe was provided by Margarita Arriaga, owner of the Mansión Iturbe Bed & Breakfast Hotel in Pátzcuaro, Michoacán. The hotel's restaurant, Doña Paca, is named for Margarita's great grandmother, the original owner of the 17th-century building. This stew is a specialty of the Purépecha Plateau area of Michoacán.

> 10 CUPS WATER
>
> 5 POUNDS BEEF SHANK (WITH BONE), CUT INTO 1½-INCH PIECES
>
> 1 CLOVE GARLIC, CUT IN HALF
>
> 1 SMALL ONION, CUT IN HALF
>
> 2 *XOCONOSTLE* CACTUS FRUITS,* PEELED AND SLICED
>
> 2 EARS FRESH CORN, CUT INTO 1½-INCH ROUNDS
>
> 1 SPRIG FRESH *EPAZOTE**
>
> ¼ TEASPOON THYME
>
> ¼ TEASPOON MARJORAM
>
> 1 TEASPOON SALT
>
> ½ TEASPOON BLACK PEPPER
>
> ½ TEASPOON CUMIN
>
> 4 *GUAJILLO* CHILES,* OR TO TASTE, STEMMED, SEEDED AND DEVEINED
>
> 4 *PASILLA* CHILES,* OR TO TASTE, STEMMED, SEEDED AND DEVEINED
>
> ½ CUP HOT WATER FOR SOAKING CHILES
>
> 3 MEDIUM POTATOES, SLICED
>
> 3 MEDIUM CHAYOTE SQUASH,* SLICED

[Churipo Doña Paca, *continued*]

Put water, meat, bones, cactus fruit, corn, onion, garlic, spices and salt in a large pan. Bring to a boil, then simmer for about 1 hour, or until meat is tender. Put chiles in hot water and set aside. When meat is done, cut chiles into small pieces and add with soaking liquid to simmering stew. Add potatoes and squash, and boil for 10 minutes, or until done. Remove bones and serve hot, garnished with chopped cilantro. Plain *corundas,* the irregular polyhedron-shaped *tamales* of Michoacán, traditionally accompany this dish.

*Available at markets carrying Hispanic foods; also see *Resources* (p. 61) for online suppliers of Mexican foods.

Pollo Almendrado Verde

Green chicken with almonds. Serves 6.

Reprinted by permission of M. Evans & Co, Inc., from *The Complete Book of Mexican Cooking* by Elisabeth Lambert Ortiz; copyright © 1967 by Elisabeth Lambert Ortiz.

> 2 TABLESPOONS OLIVE OIL
>
> 2 TABLESPOONS BUTTER
>
> 1 3½–4-POUND CHICKEN, CUT INTO SERVING PIECES
>
> 1 LARGE ONION, FINELY CHOPPED
>
> 1 CLOVE GARLIC, CHOPPED
>
> 1 CUP CHICKEN STOCK, OR CANNED CONDENSED BROTH
>
> ½ CUP ORANGE JUICE
>
> ½ CUP DRY SHERRY
>
> SALT AND FRESHLY GROUND PEPPER TO TASTE
>
> 1 CUP ALMONDS, BLANCHED
>
> 1 10-OUNCE CAN MEXICAN GREEN TOMATOES (TOMATILLOS)
>
> ½ CUP FRESH CILANTRO

Heat oil and butter in a skillet and sauté chicken pieces until golden. Place pieces in a heavy, flameproof casserole that has a lid. Sauté onion and garlic in oil and butter that remains in pan until onion is clear. Add to casserole with chicken broth, orange juice, sherry, and salt and pepper to taste; cook over a very low heat, covered, until chicken is tender when pierced with a fork—about 1 hour.

Pulverize almonds in blender, ½ cup at a time; drain green tomatoes, reserving liquid from can. Blend tomatoes and cilantro in blender for a second or two; add both the almonds and tomatoes to the casserole and simmer gently for 5 minutes. The sauce should be slightly thicker than heavy cream. If it needs thinning, use some reserved liquid from canned tomatoes.

Mole Poblano

Chicken in a rich, complex chile sauce. Serves 8.

The recipe for this famous dish was provided by Maria Luisa Enríquez Enríquez, who runs a cooking school at the restaurant Las Chinas de Puebla, located in the tourist office in Puebla.

> *Meat*
>
> 2 CHICKENS, CUT INTO SERVING PIECES
>
> 2 LARGE ONIONS, QUARTERED
>
> 8 CLOVES GARLIC
>
> SALT TO TASTE
>
> *Sauce*
>
> 2 *TORTILLAS*
>
> 8 OUNCES *MULATO* CHILES,* STEMMED, SEEDED AND DEVEINED
>
> 4 OUNCES *ANCHO* CHILES,* STEMMED, SEEDED AND DEVEINED
>
> 1 OUNCE *PASILLA* CHILES,* STEMMED, SEEDED AND DEVEINED
>
> 1 OUNCE *CHIPOTLE* CHILES,* STEMMED, SEEDED AND DEVEINED
>
> 1 CUP OIL, OR MORE, AS NEEDED
>
> 1 SLICE WHITE BREAD
>
> 2 OUNCES SESAME SEEDS
>
> 4 OUNCES PEANUTS
>
> 4 OUNCES ALMONDS
>
> 4 OUNCES RAISINS
>
> 1 MEDIUM ONION
>
> 1 LARGE HEAD GARLIC
>
> 1½ OUNCES CINNAMON STICKS
>
> 1 OUNCE WHOLE CLOVES
>
> 1 OUNCE STAR ANISE
>
> 1 OUNCE BLACK PEPPERCORNS
>
> 1 LARGE PLANTAIN, SLICED CROSS-WISE
>
> ½ TABLET MEXICAN CHOCOLATE (ABOUT 1½ OUNCES),* CHOPPED
>
> 4 OUNCES UNREFINED SUGAR (*PILONCILLO*)*
>
> SALT TO TASTE

Put chicken into a large stock pot, cover with water and add onions, garlic and salt. Bring to a boil and reduce heat. Simmer for 1 hour or until chicken is done.

[Mole Poblano, *continued*]

Reserve chicken and chicken stock. To make sauce, toast 1 *tortilla* in a heavy iron skillet until charred. Set aside. In same skillet toast chiles until they change color. Put in hot water and set aside. Add ½ cup oil to skillet and fry bread until golden on each side. Remove, drain on paper towels and set aside. Use this oil to sequentially toast until golden the sesame seeds (reserve some for garnish), almonds, peanuts, raisins (until swollen), whole onion, garlic head and plantain slices. Add more oil if necessary. Set each fried ingredient aside after frying. Peel onion and garlic.

In a blender, purée charred *tortilla,* fresh *tortilla,* bread, sesame seeds, peanuts, almonds, onion, garlic, cinnamon, cloves, anise and peppercorns with enough water to create a smooth sauce. Add toasted chiles, a few at a time, and continue to purée, adding water as needed. Add plantains and blend until smooth.

Pour ¼ cup oil into a heavy saucepan or flameproof casserole. Add purée and cook over high heat for 5 minutes, stirring often. Reduce heat to slow simmer and add chocolate and sugar. Cook for two hours, stirring occasionally to prevent sticking or burning. The sauce should thicken and reduce to a smooth paste. Add salt to taste.

To make sauce from paste, mix 2 cups paste with 2 quarts chicken stock. Add boiled chicken pieces and simmer until meat is heated through. Serve topped with toasted sesame seeds. Cool remaining paste and refrigerate or freeze for future use.

*Available at markets carrying Hispanic foods; also see *Resources* (p. 61) for online suppliers of Mexican foods.

Birria

Kid or lamb with guajillo *and* ancho *chile broth*. Serves 12.

The recipe for this dish was reprinted by permission of St. Martin's Press, Incorporated, from *A Cook's Tour of Mexico* by Nancy Zaslavsky; copyright © 1995 by Nancy Zaslavsky. *Birria* is a specialty of west-central Mexico, especially Guadalajara, and traditionally is slow-cooked in a pit oven lined with *maguey* leaves.

Adobo *marinade*

2 LAMB LEGS, OR KID HINDQUARTERS, ABOUT 8 POUNDS TOTAL

10 *GUAJILLO* CHILES,*

6 *ANCHO* CHILES*

8 CLOVES GARLIC, PEELED

2 TOMATOES

1 TABLESPOON BLACK PEPPERCORNS

½ TEASPOON CUMIN SEED

4 WHOLE CLOVES

2 LARGE SPRIGS (OR 2 TEASPOONS DRIED) THYME

2 SPRIGS (OR 2 TEASPOONS DRIED) MEXICAN OREGANO*

4 BAY LEAVES

3 TABLESPOONS VEGETABLE OIL

¼ CUP CIDER VINEGAR

1 TEASPOON SALT, OR TO TASTE

½ CUP *TEQUILA* OR *MEZCAL*

4 CUPS CHICKEN OR MEAT BROTH, OR USE CHICKEN BOUILLON

12 SMALL LIMES, CUT IN HALF

One day in advance, partially bone kid or lamb, or have your butcher do it for you. Cut meat into large chunks (some bone left on makes for a more tasty broth). Prick all over with a small sharp knife and put meat into a deep, lidded roasting pan or Dutch oven. Stem and seed chiles. Toast in a skillet until they release their scents and change color. Toast garlic cloves and tomatoes until they become blistered and blackened. Put tomatoes in a plastic bag for a few minutes to "sweat" and loosen their skins. Peel, then purée with garlic in a blender. Put toasted chiles, peppercorns, cumin seed, cloves, thyme, oregano and bay leaves in blender. Add ¼ cup water and purée, scrape sides with rubber spatula and continue to purée until smooth.

Heat oil in a deep pot. Add chile mixture (it splatters!), cook for 1 minute, then reduce the heat, and simmer uncovered for 15 minutes until it thickens. Add 1 tablespoon of vinegar and salt, stirring. Continue adding remaining vinegar plus *tequila* or *mezcal,* blending until smooth. Pour over meat and rub in marinade. Pour broth around meat. Cover and let marinate 24 hours in refrigerator.

Next day, preheat oven to 375°F. Be sure lid is secure; weigh it down if necessary to keep steam from escaping. Bake for 2½ hours. Remove only very large bones. Spoon meat into individual bowls and ladle some broth over each portion. Serve with limes.

*Available at markets carrying Hispanic foods; also see *Resources* (p. 61) for online suppliers of Mexican foods.

Pescado en Mezcal con Salsa de Frijoles Negros

Del Maguey glazed sea bass. Serves 4.

This recipe was provided by Chef Joseph Wrede. He uses sea bass in this popular fish dish at his restaurant, Joseph's Table, in Ranchos de Taos, New Mexico.

⅔ CUP WATER

⅓ CUP SUGAR

1 OUNCE CHICHICAPA MEZCAL*

4 7-OUNCE PORTIONS OF FILLET OF SEA BASS

CANOLA OIL FOR FRYING

[Pescado en Mezcal con Salsa de Frijoles Negros, *continued*]

> 1 CORN *TORTILLA*
>
> SALT
>
> 2 CUPS COOKED BLACK BEANS
>
> 1 CUP COOKED CORN KERNELS
>
> 2 TABLESPOONS *JALAPEÑO* CHILES,* MINCED
>
> 6 TABLESPOONS RED BELL PEPPERS, DICED
>
> 2 TEASPOONS CHICHICAPA MEZCAL*
>
> 2 TEASPOONS LIME JUICE
>
> 2 CLOVES GARLIC, MINCED
>
> CILANTRO AND SALT TO TASTE

To make glaze, bring sugar and water to boil. Add *mezcal* and return to a boil. Then simmer 8 minutes and set aside.

Sear fish fillets in hot pan, 4 minutes per side. Pour 3–4 tablespoons of glaze over fish. Slice *tortilla* lengthwise, and fry in oil until golden. Remove and salt.

To make sauce, mix together in a bowl the beans, corn, chiles, *mezcal,* lime juice, garlic, cilantro and salt. Put sauce on individual serving plates. Place fish on top of sauce and garnish with *tortilla* chips.

*Del Maguey, Ltd. Co., Single Village Mezcal is made in Oaxaca and is available in the United States.

DESSERTS

Arroz con Leche y Chocolate Yucateco

Maricel Presilla's Yucatecan rice chocolate pudding with achiote. Serves 16.

This recipe was provided by Maricel Presilla, PhD, a culinary historian and author specializing in the cuisines of Latin America and Spain, from her forthcoming cookbook about Latin American foods for Scribner. From Yucatán, the land that enthroned *achiote,* the saffron of the tropics, comes the inspiration for this marvelous rice pudding. This creamy stove-top dessert is dyed orange-red with an *achiote* infusion, which gives it a slight nutty flavor. Perfumed bittersweet chocolate gives it a satiny texture and a wonderful caramel color not unlike Mexican *cajeta.*

> Achiote *infusion*
>
> 1 CUP *ACHIOTE* SEEDS*
>
> 8 CUPS WATER
>
> *Pudding*
>
> 1 CUP SHORT GRAIN RICE, PREFERABLY SPANISH

8 CUPS *ACHIOTE* INFUSION

2 TEASPOONS SALT

SPICE BAG: 4 STAR ANISE, 12 ALLSPICE BERRIES, 4 CINNAMON STICKS†

3 CUPS WHOLE MILK

2 14-OUNCE CANS CONDENSED MILK

3 OUNCES BUCARE BITTERSWEET CHOCOLATE OR IBARRA CHOCOLATE,*

FINELY CHOPPED

For the *achiote* infusion, mix *achiote* seeds and water in a medium pot and bring to a soft boil. Simmer for 5 minutes. Strain and reserve liquid. If desired, *achiote* seeds could be ground to a paste to make a seasoning mix or steeped in other liquid for other recipes. Rinse rice in cold water until water runs clean. Place in a 4-quart, heavy-bottomed pot with infusion, salt and spice bag. Bring to a boil. Lower heat to medium and cook for 20–25 minutes, uncovered. Stir in whole and condensed milk. Lower heat and cook for 5 minutes. Stir in chocolate and mix to melt evenly. Simmer for 40 minutes, stirring occasionally, until creamy but not dry. Remove spice bag. Pour in a serving bowl and sprinkle with ground cinnamon. Serve with cinnamon cookies or graham crackers.

*Available at markets carrying Hispanic foods; also see *Resources* (p. 61) for online suppliers of Mexican foods.

†Wrap spices in a small square of cheesecloth or other loosely woven material, tied with string.

Dulce de Chocolate

Mexican chocolate balls. Makes 16.

This recipe was provided by Mary Stec, who owned La Belleza Stoneground, which made fine chocolate and Oaxacan moles in Camarillo, California.

6 OUNCES MEXICAN CHOCOLATE*

¼ CUP WHITE KARO™ SYRUP

2 TABLESPOONS KAHLUA™ LIQUEUR OR TO TASTE.

(CAN USE RUM OR BRANDY)

⅓ CUP WALNUTS, CHOPPED

Mix all ingredients together by hand. Add more syrup if mixture is too dry. Form into 1-inch balls and place in paper nut cups.

*See *Resources* (p. 61) for online suppliers of Mexican foods.

Flan Flameado con Tequila

Mexican flan flambéed with tequila. Serves 10–12.

This recipe was reprinted with permission from *¡Tequila! Cooking with the Spirit of Mexico* by Lucinda Hutson, Ten Speed Press, Berkeley, California.

According to Lucinda, a *tequila aficioncida,* we can offer our *gracias* to Mexico for the flavorings in this light and exquisite *flan* custard: vanilla and *tequila.*

The Papantla region of Veracruz produces some of the world's finest vanilla from pods grown on orchid vines in the jungle. The blue agave plant, from which *tequila* is derived, thrives in the dry, volcanic soils of Jalisco.

Flambéeing the *flan* at the table with *tequila* makes this a dessert which is truly Mexicano, especially when accompanied by snifters of a fine *tequila añejo* for all!

> 1 CUP SUGAR
>
> 1 QUART HALF AND HALF
>
> 3 TEASPOONS ORANGE ZEST WITH NO BITTER WHITE PITH
>
> 8 WHOLE EGGS
>
> 2 EGG YOLKS
>
> 1 CUP SUGAR
>
> ¼ TEASPOON SALT
>
> 4 TABLESPOONS *TEQUILA AÑEJO*
>
> 1 TEASPOON MEXICAN VANILLA EXTRACT
>
> 2 TABLESPOONS *TEQUILA*

In a small, heavy saucepan, heat sugar for caramel on low, raising temperature as it begins to dissolve and caramelize; stir gently. When dark golden and melted, quickly pour into a 9″ × 9″ × 2″ baking dish, swirling to coat the bottom of dish and halfway up sides. Use heavy mitts because it is very hot! Cool on a rack.

Scald half and half with orange zest in a heavy saucepan over medium heat. Lightly beat eggs and extra yolks together in a large bowl; add remaining cup of sugar and salt and mix well. Slowly add scalded half and half, stirring gently. Flavor with *tequila* and vanilla; strain into caramelized dish.

Set *flan* into a roasting pan and fill pan with hot water to come halfway up the sides of the *flan* dish. Bake in a pre-heated 325°F oven for about 1½ hours or until a fork inserted in the middle comes out clean. Cool before refrigerating overnight.

Unmold by sliding a knife gently around rim of *flan;* set *flan* in a shallow pan of hot water for a minute. Carefully invert onto a larger dish with curved edges. Garnish with fresh flowers or orange slices.

In a very small saucepan, quickly warm *tequila.* Do not burn off alcohol! Turn off lights and ignite the *tequila* as you pour it over *flan.* Ay ay ay!

Ante de Mamey

Rum-flavored, syrup-soaked cake with mamey *fruit paste.* Serves 8.

This recipe was contributed by Mariana Franco, a culinary historian living in Oaxaca. Her grandmother, Elena Diaz Ordaz, was both her recipe source and her cooking mentor.

Cake

8 EGG YOLKS

8 EGG WHITES

½ CUP BUTTER

3½ OUNCES SUGAR

1⅞ CUPS RICE FLOUR

1 TEASPOON BAKING POWDER

Syrup

⅞ CUP SUGAR

6½ TABLESPOONS RUM

2½ CUPS WATER

1 3-INCH STICK CINNAMON

Fruit cream

2 CUPS WHIPPING CREAM

⅞ CUP SUGAR, OR TO TASTE

2 LARGE OR 3 MEDIUM *MAMEY*,* OR SUBSTITUTE FRESH PEACHES

SLIVERED ALMONDS

To make cake, beat egg whites until stiff and set aside. Cream butter with sugar until white. Add egg yolks, one by one, and mix well. Sift together flour and baking powder. Blend quickly with egg mixture or batter will get stiff. Carefully fold beaten egg whites into mixture. Bake at 350°F in a preheated oven in a non-stick 9″ × 9″ × 2″ baking pan until top is golden and a toothpick comes out clean, about 40 minutes. Set aside to cool.

To make syrup, put all ingredients into a saucepan and heat. When it starts to boil, reduce heat and simmer for about 20 minutes. Set aside. To make fruit cream, whip cream to double its volume and add sugar, mixing gently. Set aside. Purée fruit and add to whipped cream, mixing gently.

To assemble, remove cooled cake from pan and cut into 2 layers. Remove top layer and set aside. Evenly soak bottom layer with half the syrup. Then evenly top with half the fruit cream. Cover with top cake layer. Soak top with the rest of the syrup and cover with fruit cream. Decorate with slivered almonds if desired.

*These fruits may be available in Hispanic food markets in large metropolitan areas.

MISCELLANEOUS

Huevos Motuleños

Eggs Motul-style with ham, peas and well-fried beans. Serves 4.

The recipe was reprinted by permission of Simon & Schuster from *Cocina de la Familia* by Marilyn Tausend with Miguel Ravago; copyright © 1997 by Marilyn Tausend. This dish is a great favorite throughout the Yucatán Peninsula. It was created many years ago by the owner of a restaurant in the little town of Motul, north of Mérida. Marilyn offers culinary tours to Mexico through her company, Culinary Adventures, in Gig Harbor, Washington.

Sauce

2 TABLESPOONS SAFFLOWER OR CANOLA OIL

1 WHITE ONION, DICED (ABOUT ¾ CUP)

1 FRESH *HABANERO* CHILE,* QUARTERED,

    OR 1–2 FRESH *SERRANO* CHILES,* ROASTED AND PEELED.

2 POUNDS TOMATOES—ABOUT 6 MEDIUM, ROASTED

½ TEASPOON SEA SALT, OR TO TASTE

Garnish

2 RIPE PLANTAINS

1 CUP *QUESO FRESCO** OR GRATED MONTERREY JACK CHEESE

2 TABLESPOONS SAFFLOWER OR CANOLA OIL

MEXICAN CREMA,* OR SOUR CREAM, THINNED WITH MILK

6 OUNCES GOOD QUALITY HAM, CUT INTO JULIENNE OR CHOPPED

1 CUP SMALL FROZEN PEAS, PARTIALLY DEFROSTED

Eggs

1–2 TABLESPOONS SAFFLOWER OR CANOLA OIL FOR FRYING

8 CORN *TORTILLAS*

4 EGGS

SALT

1 CUP SAUCE, HEATED

1½ CUPS REFRIED (WELL-FRIED) BLACK BEANS (CANNED)

Preheat oven to 200°F to warm plates and keep various foods warm. Sauté onions until golden in a medium skillet. Put roasted tomatoes, with all but the most charred parts of their skin, into a blender or food processor. If using *serrano* chiles, add just 1 to the blender and coarsely purée. Taste; add another chile, if needed, and again briefly purée. Add tomato mixture to onions, and salt to taste. If using a *habanero* chile, stir it into sauce. Cook over medium-low heat until sauce thickens, about 10 minutes. Remove chunks of *habanero* chile and discard. The sauce can be made in advance and reheated.

Peel plantains and cut in ¼-inch slices. In large skillet, heat oil over medium heat. Lay plantain slices flat in skillet and fry until darkly browned, about 4 minutes a side. Remove with slotted spatula, drain on a baking pan lined with absorbent paper, and keep warm in oven, along with ham and peas. In the same skillet, reheat oil over medium-high heat and fry *tortillas* briefly just to soften, about 30 seconds. Drain them on absorbent paper, and keep warm.

Heat black beans in a small pan. Lay 4 of the *tortillas* on warm plates and spread with a large spoonful of beans. Keep *tortillas* warm while eggs are frying. In same pan used for *tortillas,* heat 1 tablespoon oil and fry 2 eggs at a time "sunny-side" up or "over lightly." Salt to taste. Place 2 eggs on each bean-covered *tortilla,* spoon on a little sauce, and top with a second *tortilla.* Top with remaining sauce and ham, peas, and cheese. If desired, add a spoonful of *crema* in the middle. Place plantain slices around the edge of the plates.

Note: For a less filling dish, the top *tortilla* can be omitted. The potent *habanero* is the chile of choice for flavoring this egg dish, but it should only remain in the sauce while it is cooking, then be tossed away. If *serrano* chiles are used, they will remain in the sauce.

Chilaquiles

Casserole of tortilla *strips in chile sauce.*

The "recipe" for this dish, one of Mexico's great comfort foods, usually eaten for a late breakfast or early lunch, was contributed by Rachel Laudan.

Rachel, a former university professor, is a free-lance culinary commentator and scholar. She has published in *Scientific American,* the *Los Angeles Times, Gastronomica, Saveur* and other periodicals on topics ranging from the virtues of fast food, the problems of authenticity, the birth of modern cuisine, and why it's no accident that Mexican mole tastes like Indian curry. Her recipe, along with reminiscences, was provided in an appealing story form; we decided not to adapt it to a traditional recipe format.

Take two *tortillas* for each person (or perhaps three or four for hungry teenagers). Cut into six triangles. Put a little oil in a frying pan and fry until gently chewy but not crisp. Drain well. Arrange in a casserole. Pour *salsa verde* over triangles until well moistened but not sloppy. Bake in a 350°F oven until good and hot. Crumble a couple of ounces of cheese per person over the top and serve. You can't get much closer to the heart of Mexico than this.

I had first seen a recipe for *chilaquiles* some years before my first trip to Mexico. What a fuss for breakfast, I thought. Fry triangles of *tortillas.* Make a fresh green

[Chilaquiles, *continued*]

salsa by roasting tomatillos, onion, and garlic and blending them with cilantro. Cook and shred chicken. Combine *tortillas* and *salsa,* add chicken or pork and bake until heated through. Finally top with crême fraiche or crumbled *ranchero* cheese. At this point, knowing that my supermarket carried neither, I decided that *chilaquiles* were not for me.

This was why travel to Mexico helped. South of the border, making *chilaquiles* looks like no fuss at all. Everyone has a few stale *tortillas, salsa* from the day before, and the other ingredients in the refrigerator. Like French toast, this is a quick and tasty way of using up leftovers. If there is no green sauce, a red sauce will do, or pork can stand in for chicken. The fact is that there is no set recipe.

In the past couple of years I have become as addicted as my friend to the texture of the *tortillas,* somewhere between chewy and soft, almost meaty, the warm tang of the *salsa,* and the cooling contrast of the cream or cheese. If you want to try *chilaquiles,* start off with this quick recipe. It may inspire you to make your next batch from scratch.

Next time you know you will have cooked chicken on hand, stock up with the best corn *tortillas* you can find (flour *tortillas* simply won't do), a jar of bottled *salsa verde,* and a little fresh cheese. *Ranchero* is best but ricotta would do in a pinch.

NOTES FOR WORKING WITH CHILES

Handle chiles carefully because they contain oils that can irritate or burn the skin or eyes.

To stem, seed and devein dried chiles: cut off and discard stem end. Slit along one side and tap or pull seeds out. Cut out and discard veins.

To toast dried chiles: put stemmed, seeded and deveined chiles in a heated, dry frying pan. Toast chiles on both sides until they blister and give off their aroma. If they smoke, the heat is too high.

To roast fresh chiles: skewer chiles on a long fork and place directly over a stove-top gas flame. Rotate frequently. When skin is uniformly charred and blistered, remove from flame, put into a paper bag and close opening. After about 10 minutes, remove blistered skin under running water. Remove stem, seeds and veins as for dried chiles above.

Shopping in Mexico's Food Markets

Helpful Tips

The Open-Air Markets

Learning more about Mexican food in an outdoor market setting is fascinating. These markets, or *mercados,* usually are centrally located. A market set up and dismantled the same day, and typically held on a specific day of the week, is called a *tianguis.* Be sure to look for regional specialities. Non-food items also will be available in the markets.

To get a feeling for how purchases are negotiated, stroll around the rows of food stalls and watch the lively interaction between the vendors and the local people. There can be some haggling over prices, but you will discover that the prices already are quite reasonable. Your time would be better spent saving dollars elsewhere rather than a penny or two here. If prices are not marked, however, it would be wise to see what the local folk pay so you don't end up paying a lot more.

Food in the markets is sold by the kilogram (kilo), or *kilogramo (kilo).* To encourage sales, vendors often offer generous samples to taste. This is a good opportunity to ask for the name of an item that is not labelled. If you would like to give Spanish a try, see *Helpful Phrases* (p. 65). The vendors, and many of the other Mexicans around you, will be happy to answer questions.

Some of the more unusual items in outdoor markets are colorful spice pastes (*recados*), flavorful leaves such as *hoja santa, chepil (chipilín), epazote* and *hoja de aguacate* (avocado leaves), and *cuitlacoche,* the black corn fungus considered a great delicacy. Some may be tempted to try *escamoles* (ant eggs), *chapulines* (grasshoppers) and *jumiles* (beetles), insect protein sources utilized before the Conquest. See *Foods & Flavors Guide* (p. 101).

A Health Precaution

Don't ask for trouble. Avoid eating food from street vendors. Some serious diseases can be transmitted by eating unclean produce. If you buy fruits and vegetables in the markets, make sure to wash them thoroughly with bottled water before eating. The safest fruits are those that can be peeled. Bottled water is readily available and is a wise choice, even in restaurants. Using bottled water even for tooth brushing is a good way to avoid problems when traveling anywhere.

The Supermarkets

Be sure to shop in the large, modern supermarkets as well. They are a great place to get the makings for a tasty picnic featuring Mexican food. Many regional specialties will tempt you. And for convenience, before leaving home, pack some lightweight tableware and a pocket knife!

The following abbreviated list of weights in Spanish has proven sufficient to get the quantities we desired. Corresponding approximate weights in pounds are included.

250 grams (quarter kilo): *un cuarto kilo*   ½ pound
500 grams (half kilo): *medio kilo*   1 pound

If you are considering bringing food back to the United States, obtain the Customs and Border Protection (CBP) brochure "Know Before You Go" to find out which agricultural items are allowed. The number to call is 1-877-CBP-5511. Listen to the menu and choose the option for ordering brochures. Alternatively, listen to a taped message with the same information. This information can also be found at: http://www.cbp.gov/xp/cgov/travel/alerts/. Be aware that websites do change, so you may have to go to the CBP homepage (www.cbp.gov) and click on "travel" to get to the page of interest.

Resources

Online Suppliers of Mexican Food Items

Mexican ingredients can be found in stores specializing in Hispanic foods and in many supermarkets, especially in university towns with large foreign student populations. One generally can find fresh corn dough (*masa*), dried and ground corn dough (*masa harina*), fresh, dried and canned chile peppers, *salsas,* cones of unrefined sugar (*piloncillo*), dried corn husks, Mexican cheeses and chocolate, amaranth seeds, herbs such as *epazote* and avocado leaves, and spices such as *achiote.* These stores also sell cooking utensils such as the traditional mortar (*molcajete*) and pestle (*tejolote*), and cast iron or aluminum *tortilla* presses.

We have listed below some online suppliers of Mexican food items. Most of them have a catalog or brochure of their products. Please note the specific policies of each store; these can, of course, change over time. We would appreciate hearing from our readers if a listed supplier goes out of business. Please also bring to our attention online sources of Mexican ingredients not included here.

The El Paso Chile Co.
909 Texas Ave.
El Paso, TX 79901-1524
Tel: 888-4-SALSAS
Fax: 915-544-7552
info@elpasochile.com
http://www.elpasochile.com
Check or charge
Catalog available

Frontera Foods, Inc.
445 N. Clark St., Suite 205
Chicago, IL 60610
Tel: 800-559-4441
Fax: 312-595-1625
info@fronterafoods.com
http://www.rickbayless.com
Check or charge
Catalog available

Mozzarella Company
2944 Elm St.
Dallas, TX 75226
Tel: 800-798-2954
Fax: 214-741-4076
contact@mozzco.com
http://www.mozzco.com
Check or charge
Catalog available

Herbs of Mexico
3903 Whittier Blvd.
Los Angeles, CA 90023
Tel: 323-261-2521
Fax: 323-269-8246
https://herbsofmexico.com
Check or charge
Catalog available

Amigofoods.com
350 NE 75th St.
Miami, FL 33138
Tel/Fax: 800-627-2544
customerservice@amigofoods.com
http://www.amigofoods.com
Check or charge
Catalog available

Adriana's Caravan
Tel: 800-316-0820
Fax: 917-237-1830
Adricara@aol.com
www.adrianascaravan.com
Check or charge
Catalog available

MexGrocer.com
4060 Morena Blvd., Suite C
San Diego, CA 92117
Tel: 858-270-0577
Fax: 858-270-0578
http://www.mexgrocer.com

Grow your own Mexican chile peppers and cook with fresh (and dried) chile peppers. The Chile Woman sells organically grown chile plants, including *cascabel, chilhuacle amarillo, chilhuacle rojo, chile de árbol, habanero, mirasol* and *piquín*.

The Chile Woman
1704 S. Weimer Road
Bloomington IN 47403
Tel: 812-339-8321
chilewmn@thechilewoman.com
http://www.thechilewoman.com

This fine cooking school is a must for food lovers wishing to learn more about the cuisine while in Mexico. Contact Susana Trilling:

Seasons of My Heart Cooking School
Rancho Aurora, A.P. #42, Admon. 3
Oaxaca 68101, Mexico
Tel/Fax: 52-1-951-508-0469/0044
info@seasonsofmyheart.com
http://www.seasonsofmyheart.com

For delicious culinary tours to Mexico, contact:

CIA-VIKING
Worlds of Flavor Travel Programs
1052 Highland Parkway, Suite 125
Ridgeland, MS 39157
Tel: 800-961-9239
http://www.thevikinglife.com

Culinary Adventures Inc.
6023 Reid Dr., NW
Gig Harbor, WA 98335
Tel: 253-851-7676
Fax: 253-851-9532
http://marilyntausend.com

Some Useful Organizations to Know About

Mexican Tourism Offices

The addresses listed below are for two of several Mexican tourism offices that can assist you with your travel planning. We suggest you also visit the following website and call the toll-free number to request travel materials.

contact@visitmexico.com
http://www.visitmexico.com
1-800-44-MEXICO

300 N. Michigan Ave., 4th FL
Chicago, IL 60601
Tel: 312-228-0517
mgtochi@compuserve.com

400 Madison Ave., Suite 11C
New York, NY 10017
Tel: 212-308-2110
milmgto@interport.net

We are members of two international organizations that promote good will and understanding between people of different cultures. These organizations, Servas and The Friendship Force, share similar ideals but operate somewhat differently.

Servas

Servas, from the Esperanto word meaning "serve," is a non-profit system of travelers and hosts. Servas members travel independently and make their own contacts with fellow members in other countries, choosing hosts with attributes of interest from membership rosters. It is a wonderful way to get to know people, be invited into their homes as a family member, share experiences and help promote world peace.

For more information about membership in Servas, write or call:

United States Servas, Inc.
1125 16th St., Suite 201
Arcata, CA 95521-5585
Tel: 707-825-1714
info@usservas.org
http://www.usservas.org

The Friendship Force

The Friendship Force is a non-profit organization, which also fosters good will through encounters between people of different backgrounds. Unlike Servas, Friendship Force members travel in groups to host countries. Both itinerary and travel arrangements are made by a member acting as exchange director. These trips combine stays with a host family and group travel within the host country.

For more information on membership in The Friendship Force, write:

The Friendship Force
233 Peachtree St., Suite 2250
Atlanta, GA 30303
Tel: 800-554-6715
ffi@thefriendshipforce.org
http://www.thefriendshipforce.org

Helpful Phrases

For Use in Restaurants and Food Markets

In the Restaurant

The following phrases in Spanish will assist you in ordering food, learning more about the dish you ordered, and determining what specialties of a region are available. Each phrase also is written phonetically to help with pronunciation. Syllables in capital letters are accented. Letters in parentheses are essentially soundless. You will discover that Mexicans heartily encourage your attempt to converse with them in Spanish. By all means, give it a try at every opportunity.

DO YOU HAVE A MENU?	¿Tiene el menú? *¿Tee-EH-neh ehl meh-NOO?*
MAY I SEE THE MENU, PLEASE?	¿Podría ver el menú, por favor? *¿Poh-DREE-ah vehr ehl meh-NOO, pohr fah-VOHR?*
WHAT DO YOU RECOMMEND?	¿Qué recomienda usted? *¿Keh reh-koh-mee-EHN-dah oos-TEHD?*
DO YOU HAVE . . . HERE? (ADD AN ITEM FROM THE *MENU GUIDE* OR THE *FOODS & FLAVORS GUIDE*.)	¿Tiene . . . ? *¿Tee-EH-neh . . . ?*

HELPFUL PHRASES

WHAT IS THE "SPECIAL" FOR TODAY?

¿Cuál es el "especial" de hoy?

¿Kwahl ehs ehl "ehs-peh-see-AHL" deh (h)oy?

DO YOU HAVE ANY SPECIAL REGIONAL DISHES?

¿Preparan algún platillo regional en especial?

¿Preh-PAH-rahn ahl-GOON plah-TEE-yoh reh-he-oh-NAHL ehn ehs-peh-see-AHL?

IS THIS DISH SPICY?

¿Es picante este platillo?

¿Ehs pee-KAHN-teh EHS-teh plah-TEE-yoh?

I / WE WOULD LIKE TO ORDER . . .

Me / nos gustaría ordenar . . .

Meh / nohs goos-tah-REE-ah ohr-deh-NAHR . . .

WHAT ARE THE INGREDIENTS IN THIS DISH?

¿Cuáles son los ingredientes de este platillo?

¿KWAHL-es sohn lohs een-greh-dee-EHN-tehs deh EHS-teh plah-TEE-yoh?

WHAT ARE THE SEASONINGS IN THIS DISH?

¿Cuáles son los condimentos de este platillo?

¿KWAHL-es sohn lohs kohn-dee-MEHN-tohs deh EHS-teh plah-TEE-yoh?

THANK YOU VERY MUCH. THE FOOD IS DELICIOUS.

Muchas gracias. La comida es deliciosa.

MOO-chahs GRAH-see-ahs. Lah koh-MEE-dah ehs deh-lee-see-OH-sah.

In the Market

The following phrases will help you make purchases and learn more about unfamiliar produce, spices and herbs.

WHAT ARE THE REGIONAL FRUITS AND VEGETABLES?

¿Cuáles son las frutas y los vegetales regionales?

¿KWAHL-es sohn lahs FROO-tahs ee lohs veh-hey-TAH-les reh-he-oh-NAH-lehs?

WHAT IS THIS CALLED?

¿Cómo se llama esto?

¿KOH-moh seh YAH-moh EHS-toh?

DO YOU HAVE . . . HERE? (ADD AN ITEM FROM THE *FOODS & FLAVORS GUIDE.*)

¿Tiene . . . ?

¿Tee-EH-neh . . . ?

MAY I TASTE THIS?

¿Podría probar esto?

¿Poh-DREE-ah proh-BAHR EHS-toh?

WHERE CAN I BUY FRESH . . . ?

¿Dónde puedo comprar . . . frescos?

¿DOHN-deh PWEH-doh kohm-PRAHR . . . FREHS-kohs?

HOW MUCH IS THIS PER KILOGRAM?

¿Cuánto cuesta un kilo de . . . ?

¿KWAHN-toh KWEH-stah oon KEE-loh deh . . . ?

I WOULD LIKE TO BUY ¼ KILOGRAM OF THIS / THAT.

Quiero comprar un cuarto de kilo de esto / esta.

Kee-EHR-oh kohm-PRAHR oon KWAHR-toh KEE-loh deh EHS-toh / EHS-tah.

MAY I PHOTOGRAPH THIS?

¿Podría tomar una fotografía de esto?

¿Poh-DREE-ah toh-MAHR OO-nah foh-toh-grah-FEE-a deh EHS-toh?

Other Useful Phrases

Sometimes it helps to see in writing a word or phrase that is said to you in Spanish, because certain letters have distinctly different sounds in Spanish than in English. You may be familiar with the word and its English translation but less familiar with its pronunciation. The following phrase comes in handy if you want to see the word or phrase you are hearing.

Please write it on my piece of paper.	Por favor escríbamelo en mi pedazo de papel. *Pohr fah-VOHR ehs-KREE-bah-meh-loh ehn mee peh-DAH-zoh deh pah-PEHL.*

Interested in bringing home books about Mexican food?

Where can I buy a Mexican cookbook in English?	¿Dónde podría comprar un libro de cocina mexicana en inglés? *¿DOHN-deh poh-DREE-ah kohm-PRAHR oon LEE-broh deh koh-SEE-nah MEH-hee-cah-nah ehn een-GLEHS?*

And, of course, the following phrases also are useful to know.

Where is the ladies' / men's restroom?	¿Dónde están los servicios para damas / caballeros? *¿DOHN-deh ehs-TAHN lohs sehr-VEE-see-ohs PAH-rah DAH-mahs / cah-bah-YEHR-ohs?*
May I have the check, please?	¿Podría darme la cuenta, por favor? *¿Poh-DREE-ah DAHR-meh lah KWEHN-tah, pohr fah-VOHR?*
Do you accept credit cards? Travelers Checks?	¿Aceptan tarjetas de crédito? ¿cheques de viajero? *¿AH-cehp-tahn tahr-HEH-tahs deh KREH-dee-toh? ¿CHEH-kehs deh vee-ah-HEH-roh?*

Menu Guide

This alphabetical listing is an extensive compilation of menu entries in Spanish, with English translations, to make ordering food easy. It includes typical Mexican dishes as well as specialties characteristic of the different regions of the country.

Classic regional dishes of Mexico that should not be missed are labeled "regional classic" in the margin next to the menu entry. Note that outside a particular geographical area, these specialties may not be available unless a restaurant features one or more regional cuisines. Some noteworthy dishes popular throughout much of the country—also not to be missed—are labeled "national favorite." Comments on some of our favorites also are included in the margin.

With *Eat Smart in Mexico* in hand, you will quickly become more familiar with restaurant cuisine. Be sure to take it with you when you shop in the markets or dine; there will be plenty of items to identify. Breakfast (*desayuno*) occurs early in the day. It typically consists of sweet breads to eat while enjoying coffee or hot chocolate. A heartier breakfast (*almuerzo*) eaten later in the morning is more like brunch, and starts with fruit or fruit juice, followed by sweet breads, eggs, beans, *salsas* and *tortillas*. A myriad of regional egg dishes are available; try some of these specialties. The main meal of the day (*comida*) is taken sometime between 2 and 5 PM, and its courses traditionally follow a set order. Soup is the first course. This is followed by a "dry soup" (*sopa seca*), which is actually a rice or pasta dish. Next is the main course, usually a meat or poultry dish. Vegetables are likely to be included in the preparation, not served as an unadorned side dish. Beans invariably follow the main dish. *Tortillas* and bread rolls (*bolillos*) also will be on the table. Desserts such as fruit, candied or in sugar-syrup, custards and puddings are a typical end to a meal. Coffee will be served when dessert is finished. Restaurants offer a fixed-price, main-meal special of the day (*comida corrida*), which includes all but the bean course. If ordering water, it is wise to drink bottled rather than tap water. A light evening meal (*cena*) is taken about 9 PM.

REGIONAL CLASSIC   **abulón al mojo de ajo** abalone in browned garlic sauce. It is a specialty of the Isthmus of Tehuantepec, Oaxaca.

abulón empanizado breaded abalone.

adobera de Apatzingán sliced and roasted soft cheese, seasoned with tomatillo-based sauce flavored with oregano.

adobo de pollo chicken in a sourish, thick red sauce of ground chiles, onions and herbs in vinegar.

agua de cebada barley water drink.

agua de chía lime-flavored drink of *chía* seeds beaten with water.

agua de frutas drink made with fresh fruit pulp.

REFRESHING   **agua de horchata** chalky drink made of either ground almonds and rice flavored with cinnamon, or ground melon seeds. Also simply called *horchata*.

agua de jamaica vivid, deep-red drink made with the dried sepals of hibiscus blossoms.

agua de limón rallado bright-green drink made with unripe lime rind.

agua de piña pineapple drink.

NATIONAL FAVORITE   **agua de tamarindo** brown-colored drink made from tamarind pulp.

REGIONAL CLASSIC   **agujas de Monterrey** Monterrey's specialty of charcoal-barbecued goat short ribs.

albóndigas en salsa de jitomate y chipotle meatballs in tomato and *chipotle* chile sauce.

almendrado see *mole de almendra.*

amarillo see *mole amarillo.*

amarillo de res Oaxacan beef and vegetable stew in *mole amarillo,* a light reddish-yellow sauce, traditionally made with yellow *chilhaucle* and yellow-orange *chilcostle* chiles.

ante de mamey syrup-soaked cake with filling and topping made of *mamey* fruit paste.

aporreada de Huetamo dried, shredded meat with tomatoes, chiles and eggs. It is a popular dish in Huetamo, Michoacán.

GOOD CHOICE   **arrachera al carbón** charcoal-grilled skirt steak.

arrachera con chipotle y ajo skirt steak with *chipotle* chile and garlic sauce.

NATIONAL FAVORITE   **arroz a la Mexicana** red, Mexican-style rice fried in oil and simmered in tomato purée. Additional flavor depends on how the dish is garnished to taste.

arroz a la Poblana Puebla's rice with fresh corn, tangy cheese and Poblano chiles.

arroz a la tumbada seafood and rice dish with *jalapeño* chiles REGIONAL CLASSIC
and tomatoes, a specialty of Veracruz reminiscent of Spain's
paella.

arroz amarillo con carnitas Yucatecan rice colored and flavored
with *achiote* paste, with bits of deep-fried pork. Chefs who want
the red-orange color of *achiote* but not its flavor use a
powdered coloring mixture called Bijol, which contains very
little *achiote.*

arroz blanco rice fried in oil, usually with onion and garlic, then
simmered in water or broth.

arroz blanco con plátanos fritos rice with fried plantains, a
specialty of Veracruz.

arroz blanco de picadillo y plátanos fritos rice with seasoned
ground meat and fried plantains.

arroz con leche rice pudding. NATIONAL FAVORITE

arroz con mariscos rice with seafood.

arroz gratinado rice with tomatoes, chiles and melted cheese.

arroz negro rice cooked in liquid used to cook black beans.

arroz rojo rice cooked in tomato sauce with chopped vegetables.

arroz verde rice cooked in a seasoned purée of green chiles.

arroz verde con chiles rellenos popular Lenten dish of green rice NATIONAL FAVORITE
with cheese-stuffed chiles.

arroz verde con plátanos fritos green rice with fried plantains, a
specialty of Mexico State.

arroz verde con rajas rice cooked in a seasoned purée of green
chiles with strips of toasted, skinned chiles.

asado al pastor whole mutton grilled on a stake over fire. It is a REGIONAL CLASSIC
specialty of Hidalgo, where it is served with *salsa borracha,* a
chile sauce containing *pulque,* the fermented juice of the agave
(*maguey*) plant.

asado de cerdo roast leg of pork.

asado placero Sinaloense potatoes and meat in tomato sauce,
with vegetables on the side, a marketplace specialty in Sinaloa.

atapacua de carne de res beef cooked in a thick sauce containing
chiles and *masa* (corn dough). It is a specialty of Michoacán.

atole warm drink thickened with *masa* (corn dough) and NATIONAL FAVORITE
sweetened with unrefined sugar.

atole con arroz warm drink made of sweetened ground rice
flavored with cinnamon.

atole con granillo warm drink made with coarsely ground *masa*
(corn dough) that typically settles to the bottom of the cup.

atole de alegría warm drink made of toasted amaranth seeds and unrefined sugar, flavored with cinnamon. It is a specialty of Tlaxcala.

atole de chaqueta warm drink of *masa* (corn dough) colored black by the addition of burned husks of cocoa beans. It is a specialty of Pátzcuaro, Michoacán.

TASTY **atole de grano** warm soup or drink made with *masa* (corn dough) and fresh corn—both kernels and a round of corn cut from the cob—flavored and colored light green with wild fennel. It is a specialty of Pátzcuaro, Michoacán.

atole de zarzamora warm blackberry-flavored drink thickened with *masa* (corn dough) and sweetened with unrefined sugar.

ayocotes en coloradito large, broad beans in *mole coloradito,* a rich, red, complex sauce of *ancho* and *guajillo* chiles, spices, nuts, seeds, raisins and chocolate.

bacalao a la Vizcaína codfish with potatoes, tomatoes, chiles and olives, a traditional Christmas dish of Spanish origin.

REGIONAL CLASSIC **barbacoa de borrego** barbecued lamb traditionally wrapped in agave (*maguey*) leaves and slow-cooked in a pit. This Sunday special of central Mexico is served with *salsa borracha,* a hot chile sauce containing *pulque,* fermented juice of the *maguey* plant.

barbacoa en mixiote individual serving of lamb in chile sauce with anise-flavored avocado leaves, steamed in a piece of parchment-like skin, or *mixiote,* from an agave (*maguey*) leaf. It is a specialty of Tlaxcala.

REGIONAL CLASSIC **birria** lamb or goat marinated in a seasoned, vinegary *adobo* sauce of *guajillo* and *ancho* chiles, traditionally slow-cooked in a pit oven lined with agave (*maguey*) leaves. It is a specialty of west-central Mexico, especially Guadalajara.

bistec encebollado beef steak with onions.

bistec ranchero baked Sonora-style steak topped with potato slices and coriander-seasoned tomato sauce.

bistek relleno stuffed beef roll.

bomba see *concha.*

botana de camarón seco fritter-like appetizer of dried shrimp and chiles, a specialty of Tuxtla Gutiérrez, Chiapas.

bróculi capeado breaded broccoli and cheese.

budín Azteca many-layered casserole of *tortillas,* shredded chicken, cheese and strips of toasted, skinned chiles, with tomatillo sauce. It is a specialty of Mexico City. Also called *budín de tortillas, budín* Moctezuma and *budín* Cuachtemoc.

budín con picadillo seasoned ground meat casserole.

budín Cuachtemoc see *budín* Azteca.

budín de chícharo vegetable pudding made with peas.

budín de pasas a cake- or bread-like pudding with a light caramelized topping containing raisins.

budín de tortillas see *budín* Azteca.

budín Moctezuma see *budín* Azteca.

buhos fried intestines.

buñuelo sweet fritter of fried dough topped with cinnamon and sugar. In Michoacán, these treats are broken into pieces and dipped in cinnamon-flavored syrup. They are eaten crisp (*acaramelizado*) or softened by cooking in the syrup (*garrito*).   **NATIONAL FAVORITE**

buñuelo de plátano sweet banana fritter, a specialty of Tabasco.

burrito de machaca wheat flour *tortilla* rolled around a filling of shredded, dried meat called *carne machaca* (see *Foods & Flavors Guide*). It is a specialty of northern Mexico.   **REGIONAL CLASSIC**

burrito de machaca de mantaraya wheat flour *tortilla* rolled around a filling of jerky made from the earlike lobes of the manta ray, or skate. It is a specialty of Baja California.

caballeros pobres egg-coated bread cooked in syrup with raisins and cinnamon.

cabeza de res pit-barbecued ox head cooked in *maguey* leaves; the meat is a popular *taco* filling. Also called *tacos de cabeza*.

cabrito en chile ancho baby goat in *ancho* chile sauce, a regional specialty of Zacatecas.

cabrito en su sangre baby goat cooked in its own blood.

café de hueso beef tripe and lamb trotters stew, a specialty of San Luis Potosí.

cajeta de Celaya thick dessert cream made of caramelized goat's milk and sugar. It is a specialty of Celaya, Guanajuato.   **DELICIOUS**

calabacitas picadas con jitomate chopped zucchini with tomato.

calabacitas rellenas de elote zucchini stuffed with fresh corn.

calamares en su tinta squid stewed in their ink.

caldillo de nopales broth with chopped pieces of nopal cactus.

caldillo de puerco pork stewed in chile and tomatillo sauce, a dish from the northern state of Durango.

caldo de camarón shrimp broth; in Oaxaca, it would be made with dried shrimp.

caldo de gato broth with shredded beef or chicken, a specialty of Tlacolula, Oaxaca.

caldo de habas Lenten soup made with fava beans.

caldo de pescado fish broth.

caldo de pollo broth with vegetables and shredded chicken.

caldo de queso cheese broth.

caldo de siete mares hearty seafood and vegetable soup or stew popular in coastal areas.

caldo largo de Alvarado fish and seafood soup, a regional specialty of the port city of Alvarado, Veracruz. Also called *sopa larga* Alvarado.

caldo michi broth with freshwater fish, especially catfish or carp.

REGIONAL CLASSIC **caldo Tlalpeño** smoky, *epazote*-flavored chicken broth with shredded chicken, vegetables, *chipotle* chiles and rice, garnished with avocado. The dish originated in Tlalpán, once a rural village, but now a part of Mexico City.

callo de hacha con aguacate avocado stuffed with small clams, a specialty of Baja California Norte.

camarones a la diabla deviled shrimp.

camarones a la plancha griddle-seared shrimp.

camarones en escabeche rojo shrimp pickled in red chile sauce, a specialty of Tampico, Tamaulipas.

camarones en frio pickled shrimp, a specialty of Nayarit.

GOOD CHOICE **camarones en pipián** shrimp in ground pumpkin seed sauce.

camarones enchipotlados shrimp in a smoky sauce of *chipotle* chiles.

camarones naturales boiled shrimp.

NATIONAL FAVORITE **capirotada** traditional Lenten pudding made of fried bread soaked with syrup made of unrefined sugar.

carne apache seasoned, finely minced raw steak.

carne asada marinated and grilled meat.

NATIONAL FAVORITE **carne asada a la Tampiqueña** sampler plate of a large, thin butterflied beef fillet served with *guacamole, enchiladas,* a slab of grilled, non-melting cheese and beans. The dish was created by restaurateur José Luis Lorida, originally from Tampico.

carne asada al pastor meat roasted on a stake over a wood fire, shepherd style.

carne cocida en limón seasoned raw, ground meat marinated in lime juice, a specialty from Tuxtla Gutiérrez, Chiapas.

carne con chile colorado meat stewed in a cumin- and oregano-flavored purée of dried chiles and garlic, a specialty of northern Mexico. *REGIONAL CLASSIC*

carne con chile verde meat stewed in green chile sauce.

carne de puerco con uchepos pork with fresh corn *tamales,* a regional specialty of Michoacán.

carne de res molido con chilmole chopped meat in a seasoned sauce with blackened chiles and the juice of bitter Seville oranges.

carne enchilada see *cecina enchilada.*

carnitas juicy pieces of pork—meat, offal and skin—deep-fried in lard. One can specify the part of the pig desired. *NATIONAL FAVORITE*

caserola de jaiba y tallarín crab and noodle casserole.

cazón a la Campechana shark or dogfish fillets fried with tomatoes and *habanero* chiles, flavored with the pungent herb *epazote.* It is a specialty of Campeche. *REGIONAL CLASSIC*

cazuela voladora drink specialty of Guadalajara made with *tequila,* vodka and the juice of grapefruits, oranges and limes, with a dash of salt. It is served in a large, shallow earthenware bowl, along with pieces of fruit from which the juice was squeezed. This powerful drink is best imbibed slowly with a straw, although a large spoon is brought for the more daring.

cazuelita small, bowl-shaped pie made of corn and potato dough, fried and filled with *chorizo* or zucchini in tomato sauce and sprinkled with cheese. It is a specialty of Nuevo León.

cebiche raw fish or seafood marinated in lime juice; also spelled *ceviche.* *EXCELLENT*

cebiche de calamar squid marinated in lime juice.

cebollas en escabeche pickled red onions; it is a popular relish or garnish in Yucatán. Also called *cebollas encurtidas* and *escabeche de cebollas.*

cebollas encurtidas see *cebollas en escabeche.*

cecina thinly sliced, dried, salted beef. If ordered in Oaxacan restaurants, *cecina* will be thinly sliced pork, not beef, and will be smeared with a paste of red chiles (see *Foods & Flavors Guide*).

cecina enchilada thinly sliced pork in a vinegary chile marinade, a Oaxacan specialty. Also called *carne enchilada.* *FABULOUS*

cemita sandwich made with a semi-hard roll coated with sesame seeds. The roll, itself called a *cemita,* is scooped out to accommodate a filling of fried meat, avocado, chiles and shredded cheese. It is a specialty of Puebla.

cerdo con frijoles *epazote*-flavored pork and black beans cooked with chiles, a specialty of Quintana Roo.

ceviche see *cebiche.*

chalupa de Puebla oval- or "boat-" shaped appetizer made of *masa* (corn dough) fried in oil then topped with green chile sauce, shredded cheese and meat, and griddle-cooked.

champurrado chocolate-flavored *atole,* a hot drink made of *masa* (corn dough) sweetened with unrefined sugar.

chanchames Yucatecan *tamales* flavored with *achiote* and wrapped in corn husks.

chanchucate spicy chile *mole,* or sauce, a specialty of the Purépecha (Tarascan) people of Michoacán.

GOOD CHOICE **chanclas** sandwich specialty from Puebla made with a special water-based flat roll called *pan blanco.* The roll is sliced and filled with avocado, onion and *chorizo,* then topped with *mole adobo,* a red chile sauce.

chanfaina offal stew.

CRUNCHY **chapulines** grasshoppers seasoned with chile powder and fried with garlic. They are a Oaxacan specialty.

charales fritos tiny, transparent sun-dried fish, fried and eaten whole, a regional specialty of Michoacán.

charamuscas taffy-like candy twists.

che chak Yucatecan fish soup flavored with oregano, garlic and lime.

cheguiña *epazote*-flavored beef soup with *guajillo* chiles, thickened with *masa* (corn dough). It is a specialty of the Isthmus of Tehuantepec, Oaxaca.

cherna al Quintana Roo jewfish fillets marinated in lime and simmered in a vinegary tomato and chile sauce seasoned with cumin and oregano.

NATIONAL FAVORITE **chicharrón** crispy appetizer of deep-fried pork skin.

chicharrón de ranchero crispy, deep-fried pork skin, cooked and softened in hot chile sauce.

chicharrón en escabeche pickled fried pork skin.

chicharrón en salsa de jitomate crispy, deep-fried pork skin, cooked and softened in tomato sauce.

NATIONAL FAVORITE **chicharrón en salsa verde** crispy, deep-fried pork skin, cooked and softened in a green sauce made with tomatillos and green chiles.

chichilo see *mole chichilo.*

chichilo Oaxaqueño see *mole chichilo.*

chilacayote en pipián green and white spotted pumpkin in a sauce of ground pumpkin seeds.

chilahuates *tamales* with vegetable stuffings, wrapped in banana leaves.

chilaquiles dish of fried, stale *tortilla* pieces, green chile sauce and shredded chicken or pork, baked and topped with cream or crumbled cheese. It is one of the most popular breakfast dishes. **NATIONAL FAVORITE**

chilaquiles Tierra Calenteños fried pieces of stale *tortillas* and dried meat (*cecina*) in a red, soupy bean sauce. It is a specialty of the Tierra Caliente of Michoacán, the hot lands beween the central and southern Sierra Mountain ranges.

chile con queso chiles with cheese.

chileatole soup made with ground *masa* (corn dough) fresh corn kernels and chiles, flavored with *epazote*. Also a drink made of fermented corn with chiles. Both are specialties of Tlaxcala. **REGIONAL CLASSIC**

chiles en escabeche seasoned, pickled chiles, often with carrots and onions.

chiles en nogada Poblano chiles stuffed with a seasoned meat mixture containing candied fruit, topped with fresh walnut sauce and garnished with pomegranate seeds. Considered Mexico's national dish—red, white and green like the flag—*chiles en nogada* originated in Puebla and is available in late summer when fresh nuts are available. **NATIONAL FAVORITE**

chiles jalapeños en escabeche pickled *jalapeño* chiles.

chiles rellenos Poblano chiles typically stuffed with cheese or a seasoned, minced meat mixture called *picadillo,* covered with batter and fried. In Oaxaca, a local chile, the *chile de agua,* is used for this dish. **NATIONAL FAVORITE**

chiles rellenos de elote con crema Poblano chiles stuffed with fresh corn, and topped with cream.

chiles y verduras en escabeche pickled chiles and vegetables.

chilorio shredded pork seasoned with ground chiles and spices, often a *taco* filling. It is a specialty of Sinaloa.

chilpachole de jaiba spicy soup with small blue crabs and *chipotle* chiles; it is a Gulf Coast specialty. Also simply called *chilpachole.* **REGIONAL CLASSIC**

chintenstle Oaxacan *mole* made with dried shrimp.

chivichangas wheat flour *tortillas* rolled around a spicy meat mixture and deep-fried, a specialty of northern Mexico.

chocolatatole warm drink made of plain *atole* with a thick layer of chocolate foam added on top.

chocolomo beef and offal soup, a specialty of Campeche and Yucatán.

chongos Zamoranos cinnamon-flavored dessert of milk curds in sugar syrup.

chuletas de puerco adobadas pork chops basted with *adobo,* a paste of ground chiles, herbs, spices and vinegar.

REGIONAL CLASSIC **churipo** beef stew with potatoes, chayote squash and rounds of corn on the cob in a *guajillo* chile sauce flavored with *epazote* and *xoconostle,* a sour cactus fruit. Plain *corundas,* irregular polyhedron-shaped *tamales* wrapped in green corn leaves, accompany the dish as bread. Both stew and *tamales* are a specialty of the area in Michoacán called the Purépecha Plateau.

NATIONAL FAVORITE **churros** fluted, foot-long pieces of fried dough coated with sugar. Chocolate is the favorite accompanying beverage.

clemole meat and vegetable stew in clove-flavored chile sauce.

cocada pudding- or custard-like coconut dessert made with coconut. Also the name for coconut candies (see *Foods & Flavors Guide*).

cocada de piña coconut and pineapple dessert.

cocada envinada wine-flavored coconut dessert.

REGIONAL CLASSIC **cochinita pibil** pork covered with *recado rojo,* a spice paste made with ground *achiote* seeds, spices, garlic and vinegar, wrapped in banana leaves and slow-cooked in a pit (*pib*); it is a Yucatecan specialty.

cochito pork roasted in a marinade of spices and chiles in pineapple vinegar. It is a specialty of Chiapas.

GREAT **coctél de camarones** chilled shrimp in tomato-based broth with chunks of avocado, a specialty of Jalisco.

coctél de ostiones oyster cocktail.

codillo en chilmole pig's knuckles in *chilmole,* a black spice paste made of burned chiles, roasted onion and garlic, ground spices and juice from the bitter Seville orange.

codorniz a la talla grilled, butterflied quail served in spicy tomato and chile sauce. It is a specialty of Guerrero.

coleto asado pork in a purée of toasted chiles, tomatoes, onion and garlic. It is a regional dish of San Cristóbal de las Casas, Chiapas.

coliflor y calabacitas capeadas batter-fried cauliflower and zucchini.

colonche fermented drink made from the red cardon cactus fruit and sugar, a specialty of Zacatecas. In San Luis Potosí, the drink is flavored with cinnamon.

coloradito see *mole coloradito.*

colorado see *mole colorado.*

concha popular sweet breakfast bun topped with sugar paste cut into a shell design using a special scoring utensil; called *bomba* in Veracruz.

corico Sonora's ring-shaped bread made with sesame-flavored flour.

corunda unfilled *tamal* in the shape of an irregular polyhedron, formed by wrapping the *masa* (corn dough) with a long, green corn leaf. The pre-Conquest version, *corunda de ceniza,* uses *masa* mixed with ashes. The post-Conquest version, *corunda de manteca,* uses *masa* whipped with lard. These *tamales* typically are served topped with sauces or with cream and crumbled cheese called *queso de* Cotija. When served with the soup called *churipo,* however, the *tamales* are plain. They are a specialty of Michoacán.

costillas adobadas ribs basted in *adobo,* a sourish, thick red sauce of ground chiles, onions and herbs in vinegar.

costillas de puerco con verdolagas pork ribs in a sauce with greens called purslane.

crema de aguacate cream of avocado soup, a specialty of Uruapan, Michoacán.

crema de chile poblano y acelgas cream of roasted Poblano chiles in a purée of Swiss chard thickened with *masa* (corn dough).

crema de coliflor cream of cauliflower soup.

crema de damiana liqueur made from the aromatic desert herb called *damiana,* a specialty of Sinaloa and Baja California.

crema de elote cream of fresh corn soup.

crema de flores de calabaza cream of squash blossom soup.

crema de lima citrus-flavored after-dinner liqueur.

crema de nanche liqueur made from the *nanche* fruit.

crema de nuez creamy walnut soup.

crepas de cuitlacoche crêpes filled with corn fungus, a specialty of Mexico City.

crepas de pollo con chile chipotle y nuez chicken crêpes in *chipotle* chile and walnut sauce.

cuala custard made of ground corn and coconut in sweetened milk flavored with cinnamon. It is a specialty of Puerto Vallarta.

dulce de higo fig compote.

dzotobichay small *tamal* filled with hard-boiled egg, toasted, ground pumpkin seeds, and wrapped in *chaya,* a chard-like vegetable grown in the Yucatán.

DELICIOUS **empanada de chilacayote** turnover filled with sweetened paste made from *chilacayote,* a green and white spotted pumpkin. It is a specialty of Tingidín, Michoacán.

empanada de lechecilla custard-filled turnover made with puff pastry.

empanada de minilla turnover filled with shark meat in a sauce of tomatoes, pickled *jalapeño* chiles, olives and capers.

empanada de mole amarillo Oaxacan holiday turnover filled with shredded chicken in yellow *mole,* a light red-orange sauce, traditionally made with yellow *chilhaucle* and yellow-orange *chilcostle* chiles, tomatillos, herbs and spices.

enchiladas a la plaza see *pollo placero.*

GOOD CHOICE **enchiladas de Jalisco** *tortillas* filled with ground meat and chopped vegetables, covered with chile sauce and grated cheese.

enchiladas de San Luis layered casserole of *tortillas* folded in half to enclose some chile, tomato and cheese sauce. The corn dough for this specialty of San Luis Potosí contains ground chiles. Filled and folded *tortillas* can also be fried and served individually. Another name for this dish is *enchiladas* Potosinas.

enchiladas de Santa Clara casserole of *tortillas* filled with seasoned pork, nuts and dried fruits, covered with chile sauce and beaten eggs.

enchiladas montadas *tortillas* dipped in chile sauce topped with an egg.

REGIONAL CLASSIC **enchiladas norteñas** stacked (unrolled) corn *tortillas* with cheese and chile sauce between layers. It is a popular way to make *enchiladas* in northern Mexico.

enchiladas Potosinas see *enchiladas* de San Luis.

TASTY **enchiladas Suizas** chicken-filled *tortillas* covered with cream-based tomatillo sauce, topped with cheese and baked.

enfrijoladas soft *tortillas* dunked in bean purée.

enjitomatadas soft *tortillas* dunked in tomato sauce.

enjococadas soft *tortillas* dunked in sour cream and cheese sauce.

enmoladas soft *tortillas* dunked in *mole.*

ensalada Cesar the famous Caesar salad invented by the Cardini brothers, Alex and Caesar, in Tijuana, Baja California Norte in the early part of this century.

ensalada de habas fava bean salad.

ensalada de nopalitos salad of julienned nopal cactus paddles.

TOP *Hojaldra,* a specialty bread of Etla, Oaxaca, which is *empanada*-shaped and drizzled with red-colored sugar. **MIDDLE** A colorful assortment of fresh, crisp vegetables at the Mercado Municipal in Pátzcuaro, Michoacán. The pink- and green-tinged sour cactus fruits on the right are called *xoconostle*. **BOTTOM** Candied pumpkins and yams at the Mercado San Juan in Mexico City.

TOP LEFT Chef Silvio Campo demonstrating the art of making pit-roasted pig, or *cochinita pibil,* in Tixkokob, Yucatán, for Marilyn Tausend's Culinary Adventures Tour. **TOP RIGHT** Oaxaca's local chile, *chile de agua,* typically used to make *chiles rellenos,* or stuffed chiles. **BOTTOM** Corn, the foundation of Mexican cuisine, artfully displayed at the Mercado de Merced, Mexico City.

TOP LEFT Eye-appealing arrangement of spices and dried herbs in the marketplace at Tlacolula, Oaxaca.
TOP RIGHT Waitress at the popular Café de Tacuba in Mexico City, with a tray of sweet breads to select for breakfast. **BOTTOM** Coiled sausages and racks of goat and lamb roasting on spits at a large, open-air restaurant in the village of La Laja near Guadalajara, Jalisco.

TOP LEFT Women selling flowers and colorfully decorated ceramic bowls at the marketplace in Tlacolula, Oaxaca. **TOP RIGHT** Vendor at the Mercado Municipal Lucas de Gálvez in Mérida, Yucatán, building a huge mound of *recado rojo,* the brick-red Yucatecan spice paste made with spices, garlic, vinegar and ground *achiote* (annatto) seeds. **BOTTOM** Luscious fruit at the Mercado San Juan in Mexico City. The oval green fruit with the bumpy surface is the tasty *cherimoya.*

TOP LEFT *Mulitas,* small *tortillas* filled with chicken and served with *guacamole*. It is a traditional dish of Michoacán, and one of several delicious local specialties made at the Doña Paca Café in Pátzcuaro. **TOP RIGHT** Maroon pods containing flat, green seeds called *guaje,* which are eaten raw or used to make a sauce called *guasmole*. **BOTTOM** Popular snack called *chicharrón,* made of pork skin boiled in lard.

TOP LEFT Popular breakfast dish called *huevos divorciados,* or divorced eggs, served at the Camino Real Hotel in Oaxaca. **TOP RIGHT** Round slabs of unrefined dark-brown sugar in the marketplace in Tlacolula, Oaxaca. **BOTTOM** Santa Rosa Convent's lovely tiled kitchen in Puebla, where nuns created some of Mexico's celebrated dishes such as *mole* Poblano and *chiles en nogada* (chiles in walnut sauce).

TOP LEFT Ropes of *chorizo* in Toluca, Mexico, the sausage capital of the country. The green variety, *chorizo verde,* gets its color from fresh green chiles, tomatillos and cilantro. When not tied into links it is called *longaniza*. **TOP RIGHT** Cutting meat at Birriería las 9 Esquinas, a restaurant in Guadalajara specializing in *barbacoa* (barbecued lamb) and *birria* (goat marinated in vinegary chile sauce). **BOTTOM** The makings for *macum de mero,* a Yucatecan dish of fish basted in a vinegary sauce with *habanero* chiles and *achiote* (annatto) paste, made by chef Patricia Quintana (see cover).

TOP Individual servings of lamb in chile sauce, wrapped in *mixiote,* the skin of *maguey* leaves, made at Las Chinas de Puebla restaurant in Puebla.   **MIDDLE** *Chiles rellenos,* or stuffed chiles, made at La Calle de Alcalá restaurant in Oaxaca.   **BOTTOM** A dish with *mole colorado,* one of Oaxaca's famous sauces, and refried (well-fried) beans, made at the El Topil restaurant in Oaxaca.

ensalada mixta mixed salad.

entomatadas soft *tortillas* dunked in tomatillo sauce.

escabeche de cebollas see *cebollas en escabeche.*

escabeche oriental see *pollo en escabeche.*

escamole stew with ant eggs.

escebeche de Valladolid see *pollo en escabeche.*

esmedregal a la cazuela jackfish cooked in tomato and sweet **REGIONAL CLASSIC**
chile sauce. It is a popular Atlantic Ocean fish in the Yucatán.

esmedregal en chile xcat-ik thick slice of jackfish in *xcat-ik* chile
sauce.

esquites soupy mixture of corn kernels and chiles, flavored with **TASTY**
epazote, enjoyed in the marketplaces in central and southern
Mexico.

estofado almendrado veal stew in almond sauce, a regional dish
of Oaxaca.

estofado de lengua stewed tongue.

estofado de res slow-cooked stew of beef with vegetables
and fruits, in a sauce of *guajillo* and *ancho* chiles flavored with
cinnamon and cloves, a specialty of the Isthmus of Tehuantepec,
Oaxaca.

fiambre Potosino a cold dish of cooked pig's feet, beef tongue,
and sometimes chicken, in vinaigrette. It is a specialty of San
Luis Potosí.

filet a la parrilla charcoal-grilled steak.

filetes de mojarra en totomoxtle fillets of a small, silvery tropical
fish and chopped nopal cactus paddles steamed in corn husks.
It is a specialty of Guerrero and Michoacán.

flan caramel custard. **NATIONAL FAVORITE**

flores de calabaza guisadas stewed squash blossoms.

frijoles blancos con camarones secos small white beans and dried
shrimp in tomato sauce, subtly seasoned with anise-flavored
hoja santa leaves. It is a main dish specialty of Oaxaca.

frijoles charros cilantro-flavored beans cooked with roasted **REGIONAL CLASSIC**
green chiles, tomatoes and bits of pork with fat. It is a specialty
of northern Mexico. With the addition of beer, *pulque* or *tequila,*
the dish is called *frijoles borrachos* ("drunken beans").

frijoles con chipilín black beans flavored with the aromatic herb
called *chipilín.* It is a popular preparation of beans in Chiapas.

frijoles con puerco a Yucatecan dish of pork with black beans, typically served with *arroz negro,* or rice simmered in the liquid used to cook the black beans.

frijoles de arriero mule driver's beans.

NATIONAL FAVORITE   **frijoles de la olla** beans cooked in a clay pot.

frijoles maneados creamed beans with cheese, ground red chiles and *chorizo*. It is a specialty of Sonora.

frijoles negros con chochoyotes soupy black beans with dumplings.

frijoles negros de Santiago Tuxtla refried, small black beans topped with chopped onion, chiles, and crumbled cheese, a regional dish of Santiago Tuxtla, Veracruz.

frijoles negros estilo ranchero ranch-style black beans with pork in a hot tomato and chile sauce.

REGIONAL CLASSIC   **frijoles puercos** beans fried with *chorizo*, ground cheese and fried pork skin, topped with pieces of *tortilla*. It is a traditional dish from Michoacán. In Nayarit it is mashed *azufrado* beans mixed with sautéed *chorizo* and *arbol* chiles.

NATIONAL FAVORITE   **frijoles refritos** refried (well-fried) beans.

gallina pinta Sonoran specialty stew of oxtail, pork, beans and hominy.

garapacho de jaiba crabmeat casserole.

garapiña drink of fermented pineapple juice.

REGIONAL CLASSIC   **garnachas Yucatecas** appetizer made with *tortillas* with pinched up rims, topped with ground turkey and puréed potatoes, and fried. Other topping combinations for this Yucatecan *sope* may be on the menu.

gazpacho chilled, puréed vegetable soup.

gelatina de rompope con fresas gelatin dessert made with liqueur-laced eggnog and served with strawberry sauce.

gorditas de maíz horneadas small cookies made with corn, eggs and unrefined sugar. It is a treat of Nayarit.

gorditas infladas de fríjol con salsa negra puffy rounds of fried dough made of corn mixed with puréed beans, topped with *chipotle* chile sauce and crumbled cheese. It is a specialty of Veracruz.

NATIONAL FAVORITE   **guacamole** relish of coarsely mashed avocado, chopped tomato and onion, and coriander.

guajolotes bread rolls filled with a mixture of potato and *chorizo*.

guayabas en almíbar poached guavas in cinnamon syrup.

guayabas rellenas con cocada guavas stuffed with coconut.

gucheguiña soupy, spicy dish of beef with chiles, tomatoes and   REGIONAL CLASSIC
garlic, flavored with *epazote*. It is a regional dish of the Isthmus
de Tehuantepec, Oaxaca.

guetabingui small cake of masa seasoned with dried shrimp. It is
a specialty of the Isthmus of Tehuantepec, Oaxaca.

guiso de puerco pork stew.

hasikilpac cilantro-flavored Yucatecan dip made with ground,   REGIONAL CLASSIC
toasted squash seeds, tomatoes and *habanero* chiles.

higaditos Oaxacan dish of eggs with pork, chicken and chicken
livers.

higaditos en chipotle chicken livers in *chipotle* chile sauce.

hígado encebollado liver in onion sauce.

hígado entomatado liver in tomato sauce.

hongos al epazote wild mushrooms flavored with *epazote*. It is a
specialty of the state of Mexico.

hongos al vapor wild mushrooms cooked in their own juices.

hongos en escabeche pickled wild mushrooms.

hongos guisados stewed wild mushrooms.

hongos totolcoxcatl en escabeche pickled small, wild mushrooms
that grow in Puebla.

horchata see *agua de horchata*.

huachinango a la naranja red snapper in orange sauce, a regional   REGIONAL CLASSIC
dish of Sinaloa.

huachinango a la talla grilled, butterflied red snapper.

huachinango a la Veracruzana Veracruz-style red snapper, whole   REGIONAL CLASSIC
or cut in fillets, baked in a seasoned sauce of tomatoes,
chiles, green olives and plump capers. Also called *pescado a la
Veracruzana*.

huarache oval, foot-long dried *tortilla* made of coarsely ground   TASTY
white or blue corn. This specialty of Toluca can be munched on
plain or topped with sauce, chile slices and fine cheese threads.
Also the name of a large, fried oval of *masa* (corn dough)
topped with red sauce on one side, green sauce on the other, all
buried under chopped onions and shredded cheese—a popular
marketplace item in Mexico City.

huevos a la Oaxaqueña omelette in *epazote*-flavored sauce of roasted red chiles and tomatoes topped with cheese, a regional dish of Oaxaca.

huevos ahogados poached eggs in tomato sauce.

huevos albañiles omelette topped with *chipotle* chile sauce; also called *huevos a la albañil*.

huevos con chorizo scrambled eggs with *chorizo*.

REGIONAL CLASSIC **huevos con pejelagarto** scrambled eggs with smoked garfish, a specialty of Tabasco.

huevos Cuauhtémoc cooked eggs in tomatoes and puréed black beans, topped with grated cheese. The dish is named for the Aztec Emperor Cuauhtémoc.

GOOD CHOICE **huevos divorciados** two fried eggs, served side by side, one in green sauce and the other in red sauce, often with *chilaquiles* in the middle (dish shown on cover).

huevos en cazoleta eggs baked in a muffin pan with a ham slice as muffin cup liner.

huevos en rabo de mestiza eggs poached in tomato and chile broth.

huevos en salsa de tomate verde scrambled eggs in tomatillo and green chile sauce.

huevos fritos duros well-done fried eggs.

REGIONAL CLASSIC **huevos Motuleños** *tortilla* sandwich of fried egg and refried beans, topped with *habanero* chile sauce, peas, chopped ham, and crumbled cheese, with fried plantain slices on the side. It is a regional dish from Motul, Yucatán.

NATIONAL FAVORITE **huevos rancheros** ranch-style fried eggs on a fried *tortilla*, topped with tomato and chile sauce.

NATIONAL FAVORITE **huevos revueltos a la Mexicana** eggs scrambled in tomato and chile sauce.

huevos revueltos con chorizo eggs scrambled with *chorizo*.

huevos revueltos con totopos eggs scrambled with pieces of fried *tortillas*.

huevos revueltos de rancho eggs scrambled with chile sauce and served on fried *tortillas*.

huevos revueltos en chorizo de Huetamo eggs scrambled with potatoes and *chorizo* made in Huetamo, Michoacán.

huevos Tarascos fried *tortilla* dipped in soupy beans, topped with an egg and *salsa* Tarasca, a sauce made with tomatillos and chiles.

huevos Tirados eggs scrambled with refried beans.

jaibas rellenas stuffed crabs.

jarro loco fruit drink made with the juice of pineapples, oranges, lemons, and pieces of these fruits, sparkling water and powdered chile. It is a specialty of the island of Janitizio in Lake Pátzcuaro, Michoacán.

jericalla baked egg custard, sprinkled with cinnamon; a treat from Guadalajara. **DELICIOUS**

jugo de naranja orange juice.

jugo de toronja grapefruit juice.

jugo de zanahoria carrot juice.

legumbres en escabeche pickled vegetables.

lentejas guisadas stewed lentils.

licor de nanche mashed *nanche* fruit mixed with alcohol and sugar, a specialty of Nayarit.

lolito griddle-baked, filled cake made of *masa* (corn dough); a savory specialty from Hidalgo.

lomitos cubed pork coated with *achiote* seasoning paste and cooked in a sauce of tomatoes, *habanero* chiles and garlic. It is a Yucatecan dish.

lomo de Puerco a la Veracruzana loin of pork cut with a knife to make slits, which are filled with pieces of ham, bacon and chile strips. It is covered with a paste of chiles, onion, garlic and orange juice, wrapped in banana leaves and baked.

longaniza en salsa verde sausage in a green sauce made with tomatillos and green chiles. **GOOD CHOICE**

macarrón con jitomate macaroni with tomatoes.

machaca con huevo eggs scrambled with dried, shredded beef, tomatoes and chiles. Also called *machacado con huevo* or simply *machaca*. It is a specialty of northern Mexico. **REGIONAL CLASSIC**

machacado con huevo see *machaca con huevo*.

machitos "sausage" of intestines coiled around offal.

macum de mero grouper steaks marinated in a mixture of *achiote* paste, garlic, *habanero* chiles and juice of the bitter Seville orange, then stewed. It is a Yucatecan specialty (shown on cover, prepared by Patricia Quintana, noted cookbook author, teacher and chef). **REGIONAL CLASSIC**

manchamanteles see *mole manchamanteles*.

maniados beans cooked with milk, butter and cheese; a specialty of Sonora.

manitas de puerco en escabeche pickled pig's feet. Also called *manitas de cerdo en vinagre.*

NATIONAL FAVORITE **menudo** tripe soup, touted as food to ease a hangover.

menudo blanco see *menudo estilo* Sonora.

menudo estilo Sonora coriander-flavored beef tripe and trotter soup with hominy; also called *menudo blanco.* With the addition of red chiles, it becomes *menudo rojo.* It is a specialty of northern Mexico, and is especially popular in Sonora.

menudo rojo see *menudo estilo* Sonora.

migas eggs scrambled in chile and tomato sauce with pieces of fried *tortillas.* It is a specialty of Nuevo León.

minguichi soup made with chiles and *jocoque,* or sour cream. It is a specialty of Michoacán.

mixiotes individual portions of seasoned meat in a chile sauce flavored with avocado leaves, wrapped in the tough but pliant skin from the surface of agave (*maguey*) leaves, and steamed.

GREAT **mochomos** appetizer of dried, finely shredded beef, fried until crisp. Guacamole typically accompanies this specialty of Chihuahua.

REGIONAL CLASSIC **mole amarillo** Oaxacan meat and vegetable stew in a light red-orange sauce, traditionally made with yellow *chilhaucle* and yellow-orange *chilcostle* chiles, tomatillos, herbs and spices. Pork, chicken or beef could be used in this dish. Sometimes the name of the dish includes the meat it contains. Also simply called *amarillo.*

REGIONAL CLASSIC **mole chichilo** Oaxacan stew of beef, pork and vegetables in black *mole,* a complex sauce of spices, seeds, dried fruit and nuts, flavored and colored by blackened seeds of the *chilhuacle negro* and *guajillo* chiles and burned *tortillas.* A hint of anise is provided by toasted avocado leaves. Also called *chichilo* and *chichilo* Oaxaqueño.

REGIONAL CLASSIC **mole coloradito** Oaxacan dish of meat in a mild red *mole,* a complex sauce made with tomatoes, *guajillo* and *ancho* chiles, raisins, nuts, seeds, chocolate, herbs and cinnamon. Also simply called *coloradito.*

REGIONAL CLASSIC **mole colorado** Oaxacan dish with a complex brick-red sauce made with *pasilla, mulato* and *chilhuacle rojo* chiles, tomatillos, herbs, seeds, nuts, raisins and spices, and served with a variety of meats. Also called *mole rojo* and simply *colorado.*

mole de almendra dish with a complex, rich sauce of *ancho* chiles, tomatoes, herbs, cinnamon, cloves and ground, blanched almonds, usually with chicken. Also called *almendrado*.

mole de chivo (chito) goat in cilantro-flavored sauce made with *arbol* and *serrano* chiles, tomatoes and garlic, garnished with a whole boiled scallion.

mole de maíz tostado small pieces of beef in red sauce with toasted corn.

mole de olla beef and vegetables stewed in a pot with *ancho* and *guajillo* chiles and tomatoes. Sometimes small, dimpled dumplings called *chochoyones* made of *masa* (corn dough) are included.

mole de panza beef tripe in *mole.*

mole manchamanteles Oaxacan dish made with a red sauce of *ancho* chiles, herbs, spices, sweet potatoes, fresh pineapple and plantains. It typically includes chicken or pork. The name means "tablecloth stainer," and the sauce does indeed do that. Also simply called *manchamanteles.* **REGIONAL CLASSIC**

mole negro Oaxacan dish of chicken in a complex black sauce made with *mulato, pasilla* and *chilhuacle negro* chiles, tomatillos, herbs, nuts, seeds, spices, chocolate, bananas, and blackened *tortillas* and chile seeds for color and additional flavor. The sauce is darker and heavier than that of *mole chichilo,* the other black *mole* in the group of seven most famous moles of Oaxaca. Also called *mole negro* Oaxaqueño. **REGIONAL CLASSIC**

mole Poblano de guajolote turkey with a dark, complex sauce of *mulato, ancho, pasilla* and *chipotle* chiles, dried fruits, nuts, spices and chocolate. It is Puebla's famous *mole.* **NATIONAL FAVORITE**

mole rojo see *mole colorado.*

mole Tapatío meat in a sauce of *ancho* and *pasilla* chiles and peanuts, seasoned with cloves and cinnamon. It is a specialty of Guadalajara. Tapatío means "three times as worthy," and is a nickname used by the citizens of Guadalajara for themselves and their city.

mole verde Oaxacan dish of chicken or pork in green sauce made of tomatillos, fresh *jalapeño* or *serrano* chiles, cilantro, parsley, herbs called *epazote* and *hoja santa,* and thickened with *masa* (corn dough). Sometimes dimpled dumplings called *chochoyones* made of *masa* will be included. Also simply called *verde.* **REGIONAL CLASSIC**

mole verde de cacahuate pork stewed in a sauce of tomatillos, chiles and ground peanuts, seasoned with coriander. It is a dish from Veracruz.

molletes Poblanos sweet yeast buns flavored with anise.

molletes rancheros sliced *bolillos* (bread rolls) spread with bean paste and cheese, and heated.

molote appetizer of corn *tortillas* filled with cheese and either toasted, skinned chile strips or potatoes, then folded in half and fried. It is a specialty of Oaxaca and Puebla.

mondongo dish with tripe or intestines.

mondongo en kabik Yucatecan dish of tripe in spicy broth.

montalayo stuffed lamb's stomach.

morisqueta plain boiled rice.

moronga in salsa verde blood sausage in green sauce.

REGIONAL CLASSIC **muc-bil pollo** Yucatecan *tamal* pie wrapped in banana leaves and pit-cooked. The pie has pork and chicken in a sauce called *xni-pek* made with *achiote* paste, tomatoes, onions, *habanero* chiles and juice of the bitter Seville orange, inside a shell of *masa* (corn dough).

REGIONAL CLASSIC **mulita** small *tortilla* rolled around a filling of chicken, served with *guacamole*. It is a special dish of Michoacán.

naranjas rellenas de coco coconut-stuffed oranges.

natilla thin custard-like dessert.

negritos see *salbutes*.

nieve de guanábana soursop sorbet.

nieve de mango con limón mango-lime ice.

oreja popular breakfast sweet bread of French origin; the French called it *papillon,* or butterfly, because of its shape.

ostiones en escabeche pickled oysters, a specialty of Tabasco.

ostiones en sus conchas oysters on the half shell.

pachola oval ground-meat patty flattened on a *metate* and fried. It usually is served with chile sauce.

NATIONAL FAVORITE **pambazo** hard roll filled with fried potatoes and *chorizo*, flavored with *chipotle* chiles.

pámpano en hoja santa pompano cooked with anise-flavored leaves called *hoja santa*.

pámpano en salsa verde pompano in green sauce.

pan de cazón *tortilla* sandwich filled with shredded dogfish or REGIONAL CLASSIC shark and refried beans, topped with tomato and *habanero* chile sauce. It is a regional dish of Campeche. Also called *panucho de cazón.*

pancita de carnero rellana mutton tripe filled with offal and pit-barbecued with meat, then served sliced. This dish is a specialty of San Juan Teotihuacán and Texcoco, Mexico State.

panucho de cazón see *pan de cazón.*

panuchos estilo Yucatán fried *tortilla* that puffs during cooking to form a pocket, which is stuffed with fried black beans and hard-boiled egg slices. It is garnished with pickled shredded meat and pickled purple onions.

panza de res beef tripe.

papadzules *tortillas* dipped in a pumpkin seed sauce, filled with REGIONAL CLASSIC crumbled hard-boiled egg, and rolled up. This Yucatecan dish is garnished with tomato sauce and decorated with the green oil squeezed from the pumpkin seeds.

papas con orejas potatoes and chopped pig's ears with *habanero* chiles and sour orange juice. It is a cold Yucatecan dish.

papas fritas fried potatoes.

papas fritas con rajas potatoes fried with strips of toasted and skinned chiles.

papitas de cambray al ajo new potatoes cooked with garlic.

pastel de Moctezuma layered casserole of *tortillas,* shredded chicken, cheese and sauce baked in an earthenware dish. It is named for the famous Aztec leader.

pastel de tres leches cake soaked with sweetened condensed milk, evaporated milk and whole milk.

pata de mula plate of sweet, raw black clams served with lime.

pato en mole verde de pepita duck in green sauce made with EXCELLENT tomatillos and herbs, thickened with ground pumpkin seeds.

pavo en frío slices of cold turkey, studded with bits of ham, garlic and peppercorns, in a vinaigrette. It is a specialty of Campeche.

pavo en kol indio Yucatecan dish of turkey coated with *recado rojo* (a spice paste made with ground *achiote* seeds, spices, garlic and vinegar) and roasted. Served with a white sauce called *kol,* thickened with *masa* (corn dough).

pavo en relleno blanco Yucatecan specialty of turkey stuffed with pork.

REGIONAL CLASSIC **pavo en relleno negro** duck in a black spice paste made of burned chiles, roasted onion and garlic, ground spices and juice from the bitter Seville orange. It is a regional dish of Yucatán.

pavo enchilado a vapor turkey covered with chile sauce and steamed in banana leaves.

pay de coco pie of cream and freshly grated coconut in a crust with grated almonds.

pay de mango mango tart.

pay de queso a cheesecake-like dessert.

pechugas de pollo con rajas chicken breasts with toasted, skinned chile strips.

GOOD CHOICE **pechugas en salsa de Poblano gratinadas** chicken breasts in a sauce of puréed Poblano chiles topped with grated cheese, a specialty of San Luis Potosí.

peinecillo beef chops served with refried beans and *guacamole*.

pelona sandwich of meat with chile sauce served on a round roll with a crackled surface. The roll itself is also called a *pelona*.

pesadumbre chilled, marinated vegetable plate.

pescado a la Veracruzana see *huachinango a la Veracruzana*.

pescado adobado en hojas de maíz fish coated with chile marinade and cooked in corn husks.

pescado al mojo de ajo fish in a sauce of browned garlic.

pescado asado en vara whole fish roasted on a stick over a fire, flavored by burning coconut shells.

REGIONAL CLASSIC **pescado blanco de Pátzcuaro** whitefish from Lake Pátzcuaro, Michoacán, that is dredged in flour, dipped in beaten eggs and fried.

pescado con salsa de acuyo poached fish topped with a sauce made with puréed anise-flavored leaves called *acuyo* and *hoja santa*.

pescado en cilantro fish in cilantro-flavored sauce.

pescado en escabeche de hongos fried fish fillets in a vinegary marinade with wild mushrooms.

REGIONAL CLASSIC **pescado en tikin-xik** Yucatecan grilled butterflied fish in *recado rojo,* a spice paste made with ground *achiote* seeds, spices, garlic and vinegar.

pescado frito entero whole fish marinated in lime juice and cooked in hot oil.

pescado zarandeado fish marinated in lime juice, chiles and garlic, cooked over fire.

pesuñas con garbanzos pig's feet with garbanzo beans.

pesuñas rebozadas pig's feet fried in batter.

pibipollos large, pit-cooked Yucatecan *tamales* wrapped in banana leaves. They are made with coarsely ground *masa* (corn dough) mixed with *achiote* seasoning paste and filled with pieces of chicken or pork. It is similar to the dish called *muc-bil pollo.*

pico de gallo snack or salad of orange and jicama slices sprinkled with lime juice and hot chile powder. It is a specialty of Jalisco. Also the name of a sauce made of chopped tomatoes, onions and fresh cilantro.   **GREAT**

pinto *tortilla* made with *masa* (corn dough) mixed with cooked black beans. After it is fried, it is topped with sauce and sprinkled with chopped onion and grated cheese.

pipián colorado see *pipián rojo de pepita.*

pipián rojo de pepita chicken in red pumpkin seed sauce. Also called *pipián colorado.*

pipián verde de pollo chicken in a green sauce with pumpkin seeds, *serrano* or *jalapeño* chiles, herbs and spices. It is a specialty of Puebla. Also called *pollo en pipián verde.*   **REGIONAL CLASSIC**

pisto scrambled eggs with ham, vegetables and chiles.

plátano pancle sun-dried bananas sweetened with unrefined sugar.

plátanos fritos con queso y crema fried plantains with cheese and cream.

poc-chuc Yucatecan charcoal-grilled pork in sour orange sauce with roasted onions.

pollo a la naranja chicken in orange sauce, a dish of Veracruz.

pollo a la plaza see *pollo placero.*

pollo a la uva chicken in grape sauce.

pollo a las brasas charcoal-grilled chicken.

pollo al estilo Ixtlan del Rio fried chicken and potatoes topped with oregano-seasoned tomato sauce, served with zucchini in vinaigrette and chopped lettuce. It is a specialty of Ixtlan del Rio, Nayarit.

pollo almendrado chicken cooked in almond sauce.   **DELICIOUS**

pollo asado a la Yucateca roasted chicken, marinated in *recado rojo,* a brick-red spice paste made with ground *achiote* seeds, spices, garlic and vinegar.

pollo asado en guasmole roasted chicken in tomato-based sauce thickened with puréed, toasted *guaje* seeds.

pollo con orégano grilled chicken with oregano, a traditional Oaxacan dish.

REGIONAL CLASSIC **pollo del jardín de San Marcos** fried chicken and potatoes in chile and tomato sauce, served with fried *chorizo*. It is a traditional dish sold by vendors in the garden of St. Marcos in Aguascalientes.

pollo deshebrado shredded, stewed chicken.

REGIONAL CLASSIC **pollo en escabeche** grilled chicken marinated in *achiote* paste in orange and lime juice. Also called *escabeche de Valladolid,* after the city in Yucatán where the dish is said to originate, and *escabeche oriental.*

pollo en mole verde chicken in green sauce.

pollo en pipián rojo chicken in red chile sauce with ground pumpkin seeds.

pollo en pipián verde see *pipián verde de pollo.*

pollo en pulque chicken cooked in *pulque,* the beer-like beverage made from the fermented juice of agave (*maguey*) plants.

pollo Guadalajara cold dish of chicken in vinegary tomato sauce, a specialty of Guadalajara.

pollo parilla mesquite-grilled chicken.

pollo pibil chicken coated with *recado rojo,* a paste of *achiote,* chiles, seasonings and the juice of bitter Seville oranges, cooked in banana leaves. It is a regional dish of the Yucatán.

REGIONAL CLASSIC **pollo placero** marketplace chicken, a dish of quartered chicken with potatoes and carrots served with *enchiladas*. It is especially popular in the plazas of Morelia and Pátzcuaro in Michoacán. Also called *pollo a la plaza* and *enchiladas a la plaza.*

pollo Ticuleño baked dish of *tortillas* covered with mashed potatoes and batter-fried chicken fillets, topped with tomato sauce, peas and shredded cheese. It is a specialty of the town of Ticul, Yucatán.

posi dessert made of toasted powdered corn and unrefined sugar, colored deep-red from boiled prickly pear skin. It is a specialty of Puerta Vallarta.

posolillo seasonal soup specialty of Michoacán made with fresh corn, chicken, pork and chiles.

DELICIOUS **postre de almendra** dessert of thinly sliced cake doused in sherry-syrup and covered with almond paste.

postre de elote cake made with fresh corn.

potaje meat and vegetable stew with beans.

pozol water-based drink made with *masa* (corn dough) mixed with ground cocoa beans and sweetened with sugar. It is a specialty of Tabasco. In Mérida, it is an iced drink made with *masa* (corn dough), coconut and honey.

pozole main dish soup of pork or chicken and *cacahuazintle* corn, a type of large-kerneled corn used to make hominy. It is a specialty of the states of Jalisco, Guerrero and Nayarit. Jalisco is especially noted for including pork head and trotters, as well as loin, in the soup. Look for this menu item as *pozole estilo Jalisco.* There are white, red and green versions of *pozole. Pozole blanco,* or white *pozole,* is made with clear broth. *Pozole verde,* or green *pozole,* gets its color from ground pumpkin seeds, tomatillos, green chiles and herbs. *Pozole rojo,* or red *pozole,* gets its color from dried red chiles.

pozole estilo Jalisco see *pozole.*

pozole Mixteco Oaxacan specialty of *pozole* with chicken in red *mole* sauce.

puchero meat and vegetable stew of Spanish origin with garbanzo beans and vermicelli.

puerco en mole verde pork in green *mole.*

puerco en naranja pork cooked in orange juice.

pulpos en escabeche pickled octopus.

pulpos en su tinta octopus in its ink.

pulque curado fermented juice from the agave (*maguey*) plant with strawberries or pink guavas.

pulque de almendra drink of *pulque* with ground almonds and orange.

pulque de naranja drink of *pulque* mixed with orange juice.

puntas de filete beef tips.

puntas de filete a la Mexicana beef tips in tomato and chile sauce, popular in northern Mexico, especially Chihuahua.

puntas de filete albañil beef tips in *chipotle* chile sauce.

pure de papas seasoned mashed potatoes.

quelites con frijoles beans with wild greens.

quesadillas asadas turnovers made of *masa* (corn dough) folded in half over a cheese filling and griddle-baked, traditionally without oil.

quesadillas con cáscaras de papas y epazote turnovers made of *masa* (corn dough) folded in half over a filling of cooked potato skins with *epazote,* a pungent herb, and griddle baked, traditionally without oil.

quesadillas Potosinas turnovers made of dough containing corn mixed with puréed chiles, folded in half over a filling and griddle-baked, traditionally without oil. It is a regional variation of San Luis Potosí.

queso de bola relleno Yucatecan dish of Dutch origin made of an Edam cheese ball hollowed out and filled with a mixture of seasoned minced meat and hard-cooked eggs, then steamed. In Chiapas, the cheese ball is steamed in a wrapping of banana leaves. Also simply called *queso relleno*.

queso flameado see *queso fundido*.

queso frito estilo Oaxaqueño griddle-seared slices of Oaxacan *queso fresco*, or fresh cheese, topped with a sauce of roasted tomatoes, chiles, onion and garlic.

REGIONAL CLASSIC **queso fundido** melted, stringy cheese topped with spicy sauce, eaten with flour *tortilla* "spoons;" also called *queso flameado*. It is enjoyed in Guadalajara and the northern states of Mexico.

queso fundido con rajas y chorizo a Northern specialty of melted, stringy cheese topped with *chorizo* and toasted, skinned strips of chiles, usually served in small earthenware bowls.

queso napolitano rich Yucatecan dessert made with milk, eggs, vanilla and burned sugar.

DELICIOUS **queso panela con orégano** fresh cheese covered with a mixture of oil, garlic and oregano, and baked.

queso relleno see *queso de bola relleno*.

queso Toluqueño melted cheese with *chorizo*, a specialty of Toluca, Mexico.

GOOD CHOICE **rajas con crema** toasted, skinned chile strips in thick cream.

rajas con limón toasted, skinned chile strips in lime juice.

rellena estilo Texcoco pork blood sausage seasoned with chiles.

revoltijo see *romeritos*.

riñones en salsa de chile pasilla kidneys in *pasilla* chile sauce.

róbalo al perejil con langostinos snook with parsley and crayfish. It is a specialty of Colima.

rollo de nuez specialty nut roll confection of Coahuila.

NATIONAL FAVORITE **romeritos** popular Lenten dish of fritters made with beaten eggs and dried shrimp, seasoned with wild greens called *romeritos*, which have leaves resembling rosemary. Also called *revoltijo* and *tortas de camarón*.

ropa vieja dish of shredded meat with vegetables, sometimes used as a *taco* filling.

rosca de reyes All Kings' Day (January 6) holiday sweet bread shaped like a ring and filled with dried fruits and a tiny doll representing the Christ child. The person who gets the doll must give a party for the Feast of Candelaria (February 2). — NATIONAL FAVORITE

sabana de filete beef fillet pounded into a large, oblong thin steak quickly griddle-cooked, served with black beans and hot chile sauce. The dish was created by Jose Inez Loredo, who created another well-known dish, *carne asada a la Tampiqueña.* — NATIONAL FAVORITE

sak kol de pavo Yucatecan dish of grilled turkey seasoned with *achiote* paste, served in *kol,* a white sauce thickened with *masa* (corn dough).

salbutes Yucatecan appetizer of fried *tortillas* topped with shredded chicken that is flavored with *achiote* paste and garnished with pickled purple onions. In Campeche, black bean paste is added to the *tortilla* dough to make *negritos.* — DELICIOUS

salpicón de jaiba shredded crab with tomatoes, onions, capers and olives.

salpicón de res shredded meat cooked with tomatoes, chiles and cilantro.

sancocho de verduras pickled vegetable relish.

sangrita drink made of orange, lime and tomato juice and hot chile sauce, used as a chaser following a shot of *tequila.*

sikil-p'ak Yucatecan dip made with toasted, pulverized pumpkin seeds, tomatoes and chiles. Also spelled *siquil-p'ak.*

sincronizada *tortilla* sandwich with ham and cheese filling.

sopa Azteca see *sopa de tortilla.*

sopa borracha cake doused in sherry-syrup with coconut, almonds and raisins, all covered with meringue.

sopa de aguacate avocado soup, served hot or cold.

sopa de ajo garlic soup. — NATIONAL FAVORITE

sopa de ajo y migas garlic and bread soup.

sopa de almejas clam soup, a specialty of Baja California Norte.

sopa de Apatzingán puréed cantelope and potato soup, named for the Apatzingán region of Michoacán, which is famous for melons.

sopa de codito casserole of elbow macaroni, ham and cheese.

sopa de cuitlacoche corn fungus soup.

sopa de elote de grano fresh corn kernel soup.

sopa de fideos y acelgas vermicelli and Swiss chard soup. — NATIONAL FAVORITE

sopa de flor de calabaza pumpkin blossom soup.

sopa de frijoles negros Oaxacan black bean soup with dried shrimp and *chorizo.*

sopa de gato tomato-based soup with shredded meat.

sopa de habas fava bean soup.

REGIONAL CLASSIC **sopa de lima** Yucatecan lime soup with shredded chicken and fried pieces of stale *tortillas.*

sopa de médula bone marrow soup.

sopa de menudencia soup made with chicken feet.

sopa de pan bread soup with vegetables; it is a specialty of San Cristóbal de las Casas, Chiapas.

sopa de pechuga de pollo y almendras soup with almonds and shredded chicken breasts.

sopa de pimientos morrones bell pepper soup.

NATIONAL FAVORITE **sopa de tortilla** chicken broth with chunks of chicken, roasted tomatoes, stale *tortilla* pieces, avocado and toasted, dried chiles, served over cubes of cheese. Also called *sopa* Azteca.

sopa larga Alvarado see *caldo largo de* Alvarado.

sopa marinera fish and shellfish soup.

NATIONAL FAVORITE **sopa seca de fideos** vermicelli topped with grated cheese.

EXTRAORDINARY **sopa Tarasca** thick soup made with *ancho* and *guajillo* chiles, tomatoes, beans and pieces of *tortillas,* topped with cream and crumbled Cotija cheese. It is named for the Purépeche (Tarascan Indians) in Michoacán, and is a specialty of the city of Pátzcuaro.

sopa Tlaxcalteca Tlaxcala's specialty soup with tomatoes, cooked pieces of nopal cactus and avocado with *tortilla* strips.

sopa Xóchitl chicken, rice and garbanzo bean soup with squash blossoms, named for the Aztec flower goddess.

sopapillas small, puffed up wheat flour fritters drizzled with honey or cinnamon and sugar.

sopas de uchepos Michoacán's specialty casserole of fresh corn *tamales.*

tacos al carbón *tacos* with charcoal-grilled fillings, a specialty of northern Mexico.

GOOD CHOICE **tacos al pastor** *tacos* containing thin slices of meat roasted on a spit.

tacos de cabeza see *cabeza de res.*

tacos de cazuela *tacos* filled with thick stews.

tacos de chapulines *tacos* filled with fried grasshoppers and chiles; it is a specialty of Oaxaca.

tacos de dzik *tacos* filled with a cilantro-flavored mixture of cooked, shredded meat, tomato, and *habanero* chile sauce. It is a Yucatecan specialty.

tacos de la plancha *tacos* with griddle-fried fillings.

tacos de pescado tikin-xik *tacos* filled with pieces of fish from **GREAT** fillets marinated in *achiote* paste, garlic and sour lime juice and grilled in banana leaves. The fish in these Yucatecan *tacos* is topped with tomato and *habanero* chile sauce.

tacos de pollo *tacos* filled with chicken, *guacamole* and thick cream.

tacos de quelites *tacos* filled with greens called lamb's quarters, and tomatillo and *chipotle* chile sauce.

tamal de cazuela *tamal* prepared in a dish, or *tamal* pie, with *masa* (corn dough) lining the dish and covering the filling.

tamales con rajas y queso *tamales* filled with chile strips and cheese.

tamales de chepil Oaxacan *tamales* flavored with *chepil,* an herb with short, thin, aromatic leaves.

tamales de dulce sweet *tamales* filled with raisins, nuts and **NATIONAL FAVORITE** candied fruit.

tamales de fríjol bean *tamales.*

tamales de hongos wild mushroom *tamales.*

tamales de momo *tamales* with anise-flavored *momo* leaves lining the cornhusk wrapper. *Momo* is the regional name in the Yucatán for *hoja santa* leaves (see *Foods & Flavors Guide*).

tamales de picadillo *tamales* filled with minced meat mixtures **DELICIOUS** usually containing candied fruit.

tamales del Istmo de Tehuantepec *tamales* with chicken *mole* stuffing.

tamales dulces de elote fresco sweet, fresh corn *tamales.*

tamales en hojas de plátano *tamales* in banana leaf wrappers.

tamales estilo Nuevo León *tamales* flavored with dried chiles, in the style of the northern state of Nuevo León.

tamales estilo Oaxaqueño Oaxacan-style *tamales* made of *cacahuacincle,* or large-kernel corn. The *masa* is mixed with *mole negro,* one of Oaxaca's famous sauces, and filled with shredded chicken.

tamales estilo Veracruzano *tamales* steamed in banana leaves and the anise-flavored leaf called *hoja santa.*

tamalito de chipilín *tamal* made with *masa* (corn dough) mixed with the aromatic herb called *chipilín*. It is a regional dish of Tabasco.

taquitos *tacos* rolled around *requesón,* a cheese similar to cottage cheese. It is a specialty of Guerrero.

GREAT **tasajo a la Oaxaqueña en tlayuda** large *tortillas* spread with sauce and topped with strips of dried meat, onion slices and crumbled cheese. It is a specialty of Oaxaca.

tatemado de Colima baked pork, a specialty of Colima.

tikin-xik Yucatecan dish made with butterflied fish steaks flavored with *achiote* seasoning paste and the juice of bitter Seville oranges, wrapped in banana leaves, and baked. Also spelled *tikin-chik.*

tinga de calabacitas stew of zucchini, roasted tomatoes, chiles and garlic.

tinga de pollo y papas stew of shredded chicken and potatoes with roasted tomatoes.

REGIONAL CLASSIC **tinga Poblana** stew of shredded pork in tomato and *chipotle* chile sauce.

tiritas de pescado fish slices marinated in lime juice.

tlatloyo small, oval snack made of yellow or blue *masa* (corn dough) stuffed with beans and topped with a variety of ingredients such as chile sauce and cheese, or *chicharrón,* bits of well-fried pork skin. Also spelled *tlacoyo.*

tlaxtihuille special dish from Nayarit made of powdered shrimp, chiles and *atole,* a warm drink or gruel made from corn.

REGIONAL CLASSIC **tlayuda con asiento** Oaxacan street *tostada* made with a hard, foot-wide *tortilla* covered with *asiento,* the pan drippings from boiling pork skin in lard, refried beans, string cheese and several other choices of toppings including strips of *chile de agua,* the local chile.

topada de lengua slices of tongue smothered in a sauce of tomatoes, garlic and capers with sherry. It is a specialty of Coahuila.

toro alcoholic beverage made from fermented sugar cane, which is mixed with fruit and milk.

torrejas type of "French toast" made with slices of egg bread coated with egg, fried and covered with cinnamon-flavored syrup made from unrefined sugar.

FANTASTIC **torta ahogado** sandwich made with a sliced *bolillo* (bread roll) spread with refried beans, filled with barbecued pork and then dunked in a sauce of pure *arbol* chiles. This special treat of Guadalajara is topped with onions marinated in lime.

torta de calabacita zucchini torte.

torta de cielo almond sponge cake.

torta de elote fresh corn torte.

torta de Milanesa breaded-steak sandwich.

torta Mexicana sandwich made with a flat bread roll (*telera*). NATIONAL FAVORITE

tortas de camarón fresco fried, batter-coated cakes of fresh shrimp; it is a west coast specialty.

tortas de camarón see *romeritos*.

tortas de lentejas lentil cakes, a popular Lenten dish.

tortilla al mojo de ajo *tortilla* with a topping of browned garlic.

tortilla con asiento Oaxacan street snack made with a *blanda,* a thin, soft, white-corn *tortilla* topped with *asiento,* a mixture of well-cooked pork fat and crumbs of fried pork skin.

tortilla de pescado fish omelette.

tortita de papa potato cake.

tortitas de camarón seco en salsa de chilacate dried shrimp fritters in *chilacate* chile sauce. It is a Oaxacan Lenten specialty.

tortitas de coliflor cauliflower fritters.

tortitas de Santa Clara little cakes topped with pumpkin seed GREAT
paste, a specialty of Puebla.

tortitas de tuétano small patties of *masa* (corn dough) and marrow, fried and topped with sauce. It is a specialty of Puebla.

tostadas de carne apache fried *tortillas* topped with soupy beans DELICIOUS
and a raw steak mixture called *carne apache* or *carne cruda,* made with finely chopped meat marinated in lime and mixed with minced chiles, tomatoes and onion. This specialty of Santa Clara del Cobre, Michoacán, is topped with shredded cabbage and tomato slices.

tostadas de cebiche fried *tortillas* topped with chunks of fish marinated in lime juice, and covered with a tomato, *serrano* chile and avocado sauce.

tostadas de chanfaina fried *tortillas* with pork chitterlings topped with Huichol sauce (see *salsa* Huichol, *Foods & Flavors Guide*).

tostadas de chileajo fried *tortillas* topped with vegetables marinated in a chile and garlic mixture.

tostadas de pollo fried *tortillas* topped with refried beans, vegetables, shredded chicken and cream.

tostadas de tinga fried *tortillas* topped with shredded pork and GOOD CHOICE
chorizo in tomato and chile sauce. It is a specialty of Puebla.

tostadas estilo Guadalajara *tostadas* topped with refried beans, chopped, marinated pig's trotters and cheese.

trucha al cilantro grilled trout fillets in a cream-based sauce with tomatillos and cilantro.

REGIONAL CLASSIC **uchepo** fresh corn *tamal* wrapped in green corn husks. This specialty of Michoacán typically is topped with tomato sauce, cream and crumbled cheese.

vaporcitos Yucatecan *tamales* with a thin layer of *masa* (corn dough) wrapped around a filling and steamed in banana leaves.

verde see *mole verde*.

vitualla beef stew with fruit and rice.

ximbo fish cooked in *maguey* leaves, a preparation of Hidalgo.

xni-pek see *muc-bil pollo*.

FABULOUS **yemas reales** dessert of baked egg yolks in cinnamon-flavored syrup with raisins, a specialty of Puebla.

Foods & Flavors Guide

This chapter is a comprehensive list of foods, spices, kitchen utensils and cooking terminology in Spanish, with English translations. The list will be helpful in interpreting menus since it is impossible to cover all the flavors or combinations possible for certain dishes. It will also be useful for shopping in both supermarkets and the lively and fascinating outdoor markets.

a la albañil bricklayer's style, topped with *chipotle* chile sauce.

a la cazadora hunter's style.

a la Mexicana with tomatoes, onions and chiles.

a la olla cooked in a clay pot.

a la parrilla grilled.

a la plancha griddle-seared.

a la ranchera with piquant tomato and chile sauce.

a la talla butterflied and grilled.

a la Veracruzana in a sauce of tomatoes, chiles, olives, capers and herbs. Veracruz is especially famous for its red snapper cooked in this sauce.

abulón abalone.

acamaya see *langostino*.

aceite oil.

aceite de ajonjolí sesame oil.

aceite de oliva olive oil.

aceituna olive.

acelgas Swiss chard.

achiote small, hard red seeds from the berry-like fruit of the annatto tree used to flavor and give a red-orange color to meat and fish dishes, and sauces, particularly in the Yucatán. Seeds are ground and mixed with other spices, garlic and juice from the bitter Seville orange to make a paste, or *recado* (see this *Guide*). The seeds are also used to color cheese.

achoque smooth-skinned, larval salamander, a food item on pre-Conquest menus, which is enjoyed cooked whole in Michoacán. In the rest of Mexico, this creature is called an *axolotl*.

acitrón crystallized candy made from the biznaga cactus, typically formed into bars. It is an ingredient in minced meat mixtures, or *picadillos,* used for stuffings and in sweet breads, primarily in central Mexico.

acosil tiny freshwater crayfish, popular in Toluca as an appetizer.

acuyo see *hoja santa.*

adobado basted in a coating of *adobo* (see below) and grilled.

adobo somewhat sour, thick red sauce of ground chiles, onions and herbs in vinegar, typically used for seasoning or marinating meats and fish.

adobo de achiote see *recado rojo.*

agrio sour.

agua water.

agua fresca water-based drink made with fruit pulp.

agua mineral mineral water; comes with (*con*) or without (*sin*) gas.

aguacate avocado. The most desired variety of this native Mexican fruit is the Hass, which has dark, pebbly skin and rich flavor.

aguamiel sweet, fresh unfermented juice or sap of the agave (*maguey*) plant. It is available as a drink in *pulquerías,* places that sell the drink called *pulque* made from naturally fermented *aguamiel.*

aguardiente de caña alcohol made from sugar cane.

aguayón see *bistec de res.*

agujas short ribs.

ahumado smoked.

ajo garlic.

ajo macho head of garlic having a single, large clove.

ajonjolí sesame.

al ajillo with garlic and *guajillo* chiles.

al ajo with garlic.

al carbón charcoal-grilled.

al gusto as you like it.

al horno oven-baked.

al lado on the side.

al mojo de ajo in browned garlic.

al pastor roasted on a stake or spit over a wood fire, shepherd style.

al tiempo room temperature.

al vapor method of cooking vegetables by sautéeing them with onion, garlic and tomato, and then simmering them, covered, in their own juices.

alambre see *carne en alambre.*

albahaca basil.

albóndigas meatballs.

alcachofa artichoke.

alcaparra caper.

alcaravea caraway.

alegría see *amaranto.*

alfajor de coco molded, two-layered candy made of cinnamon-flavored coconut. One layer is white; one is tinted red. It is a specialty of Colima.

almeja clam.

almeja roja red clam; also called *catarina.*

almendra almond.

almendrado see *mole de almendra.*

almíbar light, sweet syrup.

almuerzo hearty, midmorning breakfast. *Desayuno* is the simple breakfast, usually bread and beverage, eaten early in the morning.

amaranto amaranth, a broad-leaved plant with tiny, highly nutritious grain, native to Mexico and cultivated before the Spanish conquistadors arrived. The Aztecs popped the seeds and mixed them with blood of sacrifical victims to form idols, which were eaten ceremoniously. The grain survived the Spanish ban on its cultivation and today is most frequently encountered as street candy called *alegría.* Popped seeds are mixed with thick syrup, then molded, along with a few raisins and nuts, into flat, rectangular or square bars wrapped in cellophane.

amarillo yellow; also see *mole amarillo* and *Menu Guide.*

ancho see *chile ancho.*

angula eel.

anís anise seed.

anona see *cherimoya.*

ante syrup-soaked cake sometimes laced with liqueur.

antojito appetizer or snack, including the many popular street foods made with *masa* (corn dough) such as the *taco, sope* and *tlatloyo* (see individual entries this *Guide* and *Menu Guide*).

añejo aged.

añejo de Cotija see *queso añejo.*

apio celery.

arrachera cut of beef called skirt steak, taken from the diaphragm muscle. Popular in the North, this cut typically is griddle-seared, and often butterflied. It is similar to the cut known as *fajita* in the United States.

arrayán small, sweet, light-green berry called *pinoché* in the Yucatán. The berries are eaten fresh or made into a paste called *arrayán cubierto,* which is sprinkled with sugar and sun-dried. It is a regional specialty of Nayarit.

arroz rice; brown rice is *arroz integral.*

asadero see *queso asadero.*

asado roasted or broiled.

asiento well-cooked pork fat and crumbs of fried pork skin remaining at the bottom of a vat after rendering pork skin to make the snack called *chicharrón.* An integral ingredient of the Oaxacan kitchen, it is spread on *tortillas,* especially the large ones called *tlayudas.* It is also added to the *masa* (corn dough) used to make dimpled dumplings called *chochoyones.*

ate sweet paste made from fruit pulp cooked with sugar, typically sold in slabs. Fruit pastes commonly are served with cheese. They are named for the fruit used, followed by the suffix *"ate."* For example, the paste made with *guayaba* is called *guayabate* or *ate de guayaba.* Morelia, Michoacán, is famous for its *ates* made of tropical fruits. Look for the name *ate* Moreliano, or simply Moreliano.

atole pre-Conquest hot beverage or gruel made of *masa* (corn dough) mixed with water and sweetened with unrefined sugar. Many flavorings can be used, including nuts, fruits, or chocolate (see *champurrado* in the *Menu Guide*). Traditionally, *tamales* are eaten with *atole.*

atún tuna fish.

aves poultry.

axolotl see *achoque.*

ayocote large dried bean; purple, brown and black varieties are common.

azadura liver; also called *hígado.*

azafrán saffron; substitutes include safflower and turmeric.

azúcar sugar.

azufrado white bean with yellow markings, grown in Nayarit.

bacalao salt cod.

bagre catfish.

barbacoa meat from freshly slaughtered animals, usually lamb or goat, wrapped in agave (*maguey*) leaves and barbecued, traditionally in a pit. Avocado leaves are added for flavor. It is popular in central Mexico.

barrilete skipjack fish.

bayo type of sweet, tan or red-brown bean; also called *sabino.*

berenjena eggplant.

berro watercress.

betabel red beet; also called *remolacha.*

biencocina cooked well-done (meat).

birrería restaurant specializing in *birria,* or barbecued lamb or goat (see *Menu Guide*).

bistec steak; also spelled *bistek* and *biftec*. Also called *filete*.

bistec de pescado fish steak.

bistec de res beef steak, typically thin and tough. Also called *aguayón*. For more tender beef, choose *lomo,* or *lomito,* the tenderloin.

bizcocho biscuit.

blanco white.

blanco de Pátzcuaro see *pescado blanco*.

blanda thin, soft *tortilla* made of white corn. It is a specialty of Oaxaca.

bocol see *sope*.

bolillo small, oblong French bread roll with a characteristic lengthwise score on top. A longer version is called *pan* Francés in the Yucatán.

borrego young lamb.

botana snack typically served with drinks.

botella bottle.

bróculi broccoli.

budín pudding; cake-like pudding, often made with vegetables.

buñuelo round, crispy fritter or pastry.

burra wheat flour *tortilla* of northern Mexico, often rolled around a filling of *carne machaca*—salted, dried and shredded meat. Also called *burrito* and *taco de harina*.

butifarra dried specialty sausage of Chiapas, colored red with *achiote* and flavored with allspice.

cabra goat; also the name for *pinto* beans, which are common in north-central and northeastern Mexico.

cabrilla rockfish, a brown fish with red spots.

cabrito young goat; kid.

cacahuate peanut, typically ground into a paste for sauces or used in candies.

cacahuazintle see *maíz machacado*.

cacao seed from the pod of the *cacao* tree that is roasted to produce chocolate.

café coffee.

café Americano black coffee; also called *café negro* and *café solo;* also see *café sin azúcar*.

café con crema coffee with cream.

café con leche coffee with milk. The cup is half-filled with hot black coffee and then filled to the top with hot milk.

café de olla coffee simmered with sugar, cinnamon and cloves in a clay pot for several hours. This is a typical way to prepare coffee in Oaxaca.

café sin azúcar coffee without sugar; also called *café* Americano.

caguama turtle; also called *tortuga*.

cajeta candy or thick dessert cream made of caramelized goat's milk and sugar. It is named after the bottomless mold or box (*caja*) into which it is traditionally poured. It is a specialty of Celaya, Guanajuato, and will often be called *cajeta de* Celaya. Another name for this treat is *dulce de leche*. If wine is added to it, the concoction becomes *cajeta envinada*.

cal mineral lime, which produces calcium hydroxide in solution, used to soften the outer hull of dried corn kernels. Corn boiled briefly in alkaline solution is called *nixtamal* and has greatly enhanced nutritional value.

calabacita zucchini or squash.

calabaza pumpkin.

calabaza en tacha whole candied pumpkin or squash cooked in sugar syrup. It is a traditional offering to the departed on The Day of the Dead.

calamar squid.

caldo broth.

callo de hacha small clam.

camarones shrimp.

camarones del río crayfish; also see *langostino*.

camarones gigantes prawn.

camarones secos dried shrimp.

camaya see *langostino*.

camote pre-Conquest sweet potato variety.

camotes de Querétero confection made with unpeeled sweet potatoes boiled in sugar syrup. Holes are poked in the potatoes for deeper penetration of the syrup.

camotes de Santa Clara confection paste made from sweet potatoes cooked in sugar syrup. Cigar-shaped rolls of paste typically are wrapped in paper. It is a treat from Puebla.

canario variety of yellow bean.

canela true cinnamon, not cassia, the closely related member of the laurel family that is commonly marketed in the United States as cinnamon.

cangrejo large crab, cooked whole.

cantina bar or tavern.

caña de azúcar pieces of sugar cane chewed as candy. After extracting the sweet pulp, the quid is discarded.

cañas asadas grilled sugar cane.

capeado covered with batter and fried.

capulín wild, dark-red fruit resembling a cherry.

caracol snail.

carbón charcoal.

carne meat.

carne de puerco adobada see *cecina*.

carne de puerco enchilada see *cecina*.

carne deshebrada shredded cooked meat.

carne en alambre shish kebab; also called *alambre* and *carne en brochete*.

carne en brochete see *carne en alambre*.

carne fría cold cut.

carne machaca dried and shredded beef; also called *carne machacado* and simply *machaca*. It is a popular filling for *burras* and addition to scrambled eggs in northern Mexico. See also *cecina*.

carne maciza meat without fat or bone; also called *pura carne, carne sin grasa* and simply *maciza*.

carne molida ground meat.

carne seca dried meat; jerky.

carne sin grasa see *carne maciza*.

carnero sheep; mutton.

cascabel see *chile cascabel*.

cáscara rind; candied fruit rind.

casero homemade.

catarina red clam; also called *almeja roja*.

cazo copper cooking pot. Certain candies are traditionally made in one.

cazón dogfish or small shark; also called *tiburón*.

cazuela traditional Mexican clay casserole with two small clay handles. It is glazed on the inside only. A ramekin is called *cazuelita*.

cebolla onion.

cebolla curtida Yucatecan relish made of red onion slices marinated in the juice of bitter Seville oranges.

cebolla morada red onion.

cebollina chive.

cebollita scallion.

cecina long strip of salted and dried beef. From a thick slab of meat, one long, continuous piece is made by thinly slicing with the grain across the face of the meat, almost to the end, then rotating the meat 180° and repeating this step until the entire slab of meat is cut. Each successive, incomplete slice begins at the edge where the previous cut was not quite completed and slightly below it. Ultimately a thin strip many multiples of the length of the original slab is produced, somewhat akin to a chain of paper dolls. The meat is dried for a few hours or overnight; meat dried for at least two days becomes jerky. In Oaxaca, *cecina* is made with pork and is typically coated with red chile paste. Other names for pork sliced into long strips and coated with this paste are *carne de puerco enchilada* and *carne de puerco adobada*. *Cecina* made with beef is called *tasajo* in Oaxaca.

cemita round roll with thick, dark crust sprinkled with sesame seeds (also see *Menu Guide*).

cena light evening meal, generally after 9 PM.

cerdo pig.

cereza cherry.

cervecería bar selling beer.

cerveza beer.

chabacano apricot.

chalupa see *sope*.

chambarete de mano beef foreshank; beef hindshank is *chambarete de pata*.

changarrito popular name for fast-food stand in the marketplace.

chapulín grasshopper, a pre-Conquest protein source that is still enjoyed today in Oaxaca. Those caught in alfalfa fields are thought tastier than those caught in corn fields.

charal tiny, semi-transparent minnow-like fish sold dried.

charanda liquor made from quince; it is a specialty of Michoacán.

chaya chard-like vegetable grown in the Yucatán.

chayote pear-shaped squash, sold in markets in three varieties: white, light-green and dark-green. The dark-green variety is larger, spiny and considered the most flavorful of the three.

chepiche wild herb with long, thin leaves, eaten in Oaxaca with black beans.

chepil wild herb in cornfields, whose aromatic, short, thin leaves are used in southern Mexico to flavor soups, *tamales* and rice. Also called *chipilín*.

cherimoya oval to heart-shaped green fruit, 4 to 8 inches long, with a variable surface pattern of either small bumps or indentations resembling thumbprints. The scrumptious white pulp of this tropical beauty is sweet and juicy, and tastes like vanilla custard; also called *anona* and *pox*.

cherna jewfish, a type of large sea bass.

chía type of sage, whose seeds are used in breads and beverages.

chicharines ersatz *chicharrón,* or deep-fried pork rind, made of an orange-colored flour and water mixture, and formed into many different shapes. It is fried and eaten as a snack.

chícharo pea.

chicharrón scored pork rind cooked twice in boiling lard. During the second boiling, in hotter lard than the first, the skin expands and becomes airy and crisp. It is a popular street food and snack to accompany drinks. It is also served softened in sauces.

chicharrón prensado sheets of cooked pork rind pressed into cakes.

chichilo see *mole chichilo.*

chico small.

chicozapote sapodilla, a light-brown fruit, 2 to 3 inches in diameter, with rough skin and very sweet, yellow-brown, granular pulp that tastes like pears.

chilaca see *chile chilaca.*

chilacayote large, green and white spotted pumpkin with light tan flesh and white seeds. When candied it is called *dulce de chilacayote.*

chilcostle see *chile chilcostle.*

chile chile.

chile ancho fat, ripened, dried, slightly hot *chile* Poblano. It has wrinkled, dark red-brown skin. Called *chile pasilla* in Michoacán.

chile canario see *chile manzano.*

chile caribe see *chile cera.*

chile carricillo see *chile largo.*

chile cascabel small, round, dried, mildly hot chile with smooth, red-brown skin. When shaken, it sounds like a rattlesnake, *cascabel* in Spanish.

chile cera small, yellow, somewhat hot chile with smooth skin. It is used fresh, primarily in northern Mexico. Also called *chile caribe.*

chile chilaca long, thin, dark-green, somewhat hot chile with lengthwise shallow grooves, grown in Querétaro, Michoacán and Puebla. Also called *chile para deshebrar,* chile for shredding, because it typically is cut into strips, or *rajas,* after being blackened and skinned. When ripened and dried, it is the *chile pasilla.*

chile chilacate smooth, mildly hot chile used fresh or dried.

chile chilcostle long, thin, Oaxacan chile that ripens from dark green to deep red. When dried, it is deep reddish-brown and is used to make yellow *moles,* or sauces.

chile chilhuacle Oaxacan dried, somewhat square, mild chile with tough skin. Black- (*chilhuacle negro*), red- (*chilhuacle rojo*) and yellow-skinned (*chilhuacle amarillo*) varieties are grown. They are key ingredients in Oaxaca's famous colored *moles,* or sauces.

chile chipotle the fully ripened *chile jalapeño,* dried and smoked. It has light-brown, very alligatored skin and is quite hot.

chile chipotle mora see *chile mora.*

chile cuaresmeño see *chile jalapeño.*

chile de agua Oaxaca's local chile used fresh. This long, hot chile is green when mature and orange-red when fully ripe. It is used in Oaxaca to make *rajas* (strips of toasted, skinned chiles) and *chile rellenos* (stuffed chiles).

chile de árbol long, pointed, smooth-skinned, slender chile, which is very hot. It is green when mature and bright red when fully ripe. It remains red when dried. Ground *chile de árbol* can substitute for cayenne pepper.

chile dulce see *pimiento morrón.*

chile fresco fresh, not dried, chile.

chile gordo see *chile jalapeño.*

chile guajillo long, thin, pointed, dried, hot chile with smooth, red-brown skin. It colors foods yellow. In some regions it is called *chile cascabel,* or rattlesnake, because it rattles when shaken, but it should not be confused with the round chile also called *chile cascabel.* When fresh, the *chile guajillo* is called the *chile mirasol.* Also simply called *guajillo.*

chile güero long, pointed, light-yellow chile with smooth skin, used fresh. In the Yucatán, it is pale green and called *chile xcat-ik.* It is often pickled.

chile habanero small, lantern-shaped, super hot chile grown in the Yucatán; its smooth, undulating skin can be yellow, light-green or orange.

chile jalapeño smooth, hot chile used fresh or pickled when mature, but still green, or bright red and fully ripened. Some are called *hauchinango,* or red snapper, because they have marks resembling fish scales. Called *chile gordo* in Veracruz and *chile cuaresmeño* in central Mexico. When smoked and dried, it is the *chile chipotle.*

chile japonés see *chile serrano.*

chile jarál see *chile* Poblano.

chile largo long, thin, curved chile used fresh; also called *chile carricillo.*

chile largo colorado see *chile seco del norte.*

chile manzano round, smooth, fresh chile with the lantern shape of the *chile habanero,* but larger and milder. It can be green, yellow, orange or red. Called *chile perón* in Michoacán and *chile canario* in Oaxaca.

chile mirasol long, hot, pointed chile that adds yellow color to foods. Called *chile guajillo* when dried.

chile mora very hot, dark-purple chile; also called *chile chipotle mora.*

chile morita small, very hot, dried, smoked chile with dark-purple skin.

chile mulato long, hot chile similar in shape to the *chile ancho.* Used dried, it has wrinkled, dark-brown to black skin. It is a key ingredient in *mole* Poblano (see *Menu Guide*).

chile negro see *chile pasilla.*

chile para deshebrar see *chile chilaca.*

chile para rellenar see *chile* Poblano.

chile pasado see *chile verde del norte.*

chile pasilla long, thin, fairly hot chile with dark-brown to black wrinkled skin and lengthwise furrows; it is the dried *chile chilaca.* Also called *chile negro* in some regions. In Oaxaca it is called *chile pasilla de* Mexico to distinguish it from the local chile called *chile pasilla de* Oaxaca, a hot, wrinkled, smoked and dried chile featured in the area's regional cuisine. It is also the name for *chile ancho* in Michoacán.

chile perón see *chile manzano.*

chile piquín tiny, very hot, red chile.

chile Poblano large, heart-shaped, smooth, dark-green, mildly hot chile. Not used raw, it typically is stuffed and cooked, hence it is often called *chile para rellenar,* or chile for stuffing. It is also roasted and cut into *rajas,* or strips. Also called *chile jarál.* Dark red when fully ripe, it is dried and becomes the *chile ancho.*

chile seca powdered dried chile.

chile seco a dried chile.

chile seco del norte somewhat hot chile grown in northern Mexico, whose red-orange skin has lengthwise folds. Also called *chile largo colorado.*

chile seco Yucateco small, pale-green chile grown in the Yucatán. Orange when ripened, it is dried, ground and charred, and mixed with other spices to make *recado negro,* a dark black paste used to season regional dishes (see this *Guide*). Also called *chile verde.*

chile serrano small, smooth-skinned, bright green, hot chile typically used fresh in uncooked chile sauces. It is red when fully ripened. Although it is also called *chile verde,* it is distinct from the *chile seco* Yucateco, which is also called *chile verde.* When ripened and dry, the *chile serrano* is called *chile serrano seco* or *chile japonés.*

chile verde see *chile serrano* and *chile seco* Yucateco.

chile verde del norte large, long, slender, green, somewhat hot chile used in northwestern Mexico. Dried, it becomes the wrinkled, black *chile pasado.*

chile xcat-ik see *chile güero.*

chileajo chile and garlic sauce.

chilhuacle see *chile chilhuacle.*

chilmole see *recado negro.*

chinchayote edible root of the chayote plant eaten cooked.

chino large muffin nestled in a paper square serving as a muffin pan liner. It is a specialty of Puebla. Also the name for the orange in the Yucatán.

chipilín see *chepil.*

chipotle see *chile chipotle.*

chiquihuite traditional woven *tortilla* basket lined with a towel to keep *tortillas* warm and fresh. Alas, *tortillas* occasionally are served today in unattractive styrofoam containers, which do, however, keep them "fresh from the griddle" longer.

chirmole see *recado negro.*

chirmolera clay dish with a raspy surface used for grating.

chivo male goat; also spelled *chito.*

chochoyones small *masa* (corn dough) dumplings with a characteristic central depression made by poking them with a finger. The dough is sometimes mixed with fresh herbs.

chorizo sausage made with pork and chiles. A red version with dried chiles and a green version, *chorizo verde,* made with tomatillos, fresh green chiles, and cilantro are specialties of Toluca, Mexico, a city famous for its sausage making.

chorizo con furia *chorizo* containing *chile de árbol.*

chuleta pork or lamb rib chop.

cilantro leaves of the coriander plant.

ciruela plum.

clavo clove; also called *clavo de olor.*

clayuda see *tlayuda.*

cocada hard candy made of shredded or ribboned coconut meat, held together with caramelized sugar. It is available in several different colors. Particularly tasty is *cocada dorada,* heaping patties of coconut in a dark caramel coating. Also the name of coconut desserts (see *Menu Guide*).

cochinilla small insect living on the nopal cactus in Mexico. The dried bodies of females are used to make a scarlet dye for coloring the fillings of sweet *tamales* red; the dye is also used to color textiles.

cochinita small pig; also a pig-shaped anise-flavored cookie of Spanish origin.

cocido cooked.

cocina economica restaurant serving good quality food very cheaply.

coco coconut.

codorniz quail.

col cabbage; less commonly called *repollo.*

col de Bruselas Brussels sprouts.

cola de buey oxtail.

colado strained.

coliflor cauliflower.

coloradito see *mole coloradito.*

colorado see *mole colorado.*

colorines see *flor de colorines.*

comal round, unglazed earthenware griddle used to cook *tortillas* and toast ingredients over a fire. When new, it is cured with limestone and water. Metal ones are used on stoves.

comida main meal of the day, usually served between 2–5 PM.

comida corrida daily special, a fixed-price main meal with many courses.

comino cumin.

con with.

con gas with gas (carbonated).

con hielo with ice.

con todo with everything.

conejo rabbit.

copita tiny clay cup typically used to drink *mezcal*.

corazón heart.

corazón de alcachofa artichoke heart.

corbina corvina, or kingfish.

cordero lamb.

cos romaine lettuce.

costilla rib.

Cotija see *queso añejo*.

crema sweet cream.

crema agria cultured, sour variety of cream.

crema espesa rich, unpasteurized heavy cream.

criollo native or locally grown; wild.

crudo raw.

cuaresmeño *chile cuaresmeño;* see *chile jalapeño*.

cucaracha crayfish (literally cockroach); also see *langostino*.

cuchara spoon.

cuchillo knife.

cuerno croissant.

cuichis *tamales* wrapped in fresh green corn husks, a preparation style in northern Veracruz.

cuitlacoche black corn fungus considered a great delicacy in central Mexico. It attacks the kernels and deforms them, producing a black mass in gray casing. The fungus is used to flavor several foods, including soups, *tacos, quesadillas, empanadas* and crêpes. Nouvelle additions to the menu include dark, *cuitlacoche*-flavored pasta and *cuitlacoche*-stuffed chicken breasts. Corn grown in the United States has a higher sugar content. Corn fungus on these ears is not considered as tasty by connoisseurs and is a nuisance to farmers. Also spelled *huitlacoche*.

curado *pulque* blended with fresh fruit.

cúrcuma turmeric.

curtido marinated in vinegar; also means candied fruits soaked in alcohol.

dátil date.

de olla slow cooking in an earthenware pot.

desayuno simple breakfast, usually bread and beverage, eaten early in the morning. The hearty midmorning breakfast is called *almuerzo*.

deshebrada shredded.

doblada *tortilla* topped with chile sauce and folded, or doubled over, a popular preparation in Hidalgo.

dulce sweet or sweetmeat.

dulce de chilacayote see *chilacayote*.

dulce de leche see *cajeta*.

dulce de limón see *limón relleno de coco*.

dulce de pasta de almendra flower- or animal-shaped candy made with ground almonds, a specialty of Durango.

dulce de tamarindo tamarind fruit pulp mixed with sugar. It is sold in cakes, rolls and balls. A savory variety made in Guadalajara contains salt and chile powder produced there.

dulce en almíbar fruit preserved in syrup.

dulcería shop selling sweets.

durazno peach. Uncultivated trees bear small ones called *durazno corriente*.

durazno prensado dried, pressed peach.

dzik cilantro-flavored mixture of cooked, shredded meat, tomato, and *habanero* chile sauce, often used as a *taco* filling in the Yucatán.

ejote string bean.

elote fresh corn, as opposed to dried corn, which is called *maíz*. Also the name for sugar-coated bread made in the shape of an ear of corn, with cinnamon in the center.

elote con todo an ear of corn flavored with lime juice and powdered chiles.

empanada pastry turnover usually made with wheat flour.

empanizado breaded.

empapelado wrapped in paper.

en adobo marinated and cooked in *adobo,* a sauce of chiles, onions, herbs and vinegar.

en frío cold.

en kabik in spicy broth.

en su tinta in its ink (e.g., pertaining to a preparation of squid).

en sus conchas on the half-shell.

encacahuatado in peanut sauce, often with chiles and sesame seeds.

encebollado in onion sauce.

enchilada *tortilla* dipped in chile sauce and filled with a variety of ingredients.

encurtidos pickled condiments.

eneldo dill.

enfrijolado dipped in black bean sauce.

enjitomatado dipped in tomato sauce.

enmolado dipped in *mole,* or sauce.

ensalada salad.

entomatado dipped in tomatillo sauce.

entrecot roast beef.

entremés appetizer.

envinado with wine added.

epazote fragrant herb used in many Mexican dishes, especially beans. Red- and green-leaved varieties are available. Also known as wormseed, Mexican tea and goosefoot.

escabeche marinade of vinegar and herbs used to pickle food. With the addition of chiles the sauce becomes an *adobo.*

escamoles ant eggs, a delicacy of Hidalgo.

escarola endive.

esmedregal type of jackfish.

espaldilla pork shoulder cut.

espárrago asparagus.

espelón black-skinned bean available in Yucatecan markets.

espinaca spinach.

espinazo backbone.

estílo in the style of.

estofado stew.

estragón tarragon.

extraviado fish similar to red snapper but gray in color.

faisán pheasant.

fajita see *arrachera.*

falda loin of beef, lamb, etc.

fiambre cooked meats served cold; also cold meat or seafood fillings for *tacos,* a regional specialty of Mérida, Yucatán (also see *Menu Guide*).

fideos vermicelli.

filete see *bistec.*

filete a la Tampiqueña butterflied beef fillet.

filete de pescado fish fillet.

flameado flambé.

flauta large *tortilla* (or two smaller, overlapping *tortillas*) rolled tightly around a filling to form a flute-like cylinder that is then fried until crisp. *Flautas* are especially popular in Jalisco.

flor flower.

flor de aba beige bean.

flor de calabaza flower of a zucchini or squash plant. The male blossom is used in cooking.

flor de colorines red flower from the coral tree, whose petals are chopped up and added to several dishes, including *fritatas*. Also called *colorines*.

flor de mayo reddish purple speckled bean.

fonda small, simple eatery in marketplaces.

fresa strawberry.

fresco fresh.

fríjol bean.

fríjol blanco small white bean.

fríjol negro black bean. Small, shiny ones used primarily in southern Mexico are called *fríjol negro a la* Oaxaqueña.

fríjol nuevo new bean from this year's harvest; can also mean fresh bean still in the pod. It is said that Indian women can tell how old beans are and how long they need to be cooked, simply by breathing on them.

fríjol viejo old bean from last year's harvest.

fritata egg dish, typically with chopped vegetables and meat.

frito fried.

fritura fritter; also called *tortita*.

fruta fruit.

fruta cristalizada sugar-crystallized fruit; also called *fruta cubierta*.

fruta seca dried fruit.

galleta cracker or cookie.

gallina hen.

ganga on sale; another term for *ganga* is *oferta*.

garbanzo chickpea.

garnacha see *sope*.

gaseosa soft drink; also called *refresco*.

gaznate cone- or cylinder-shaped pastry filled with sweet whipped cream, fruit paste or meringue.

gengibre ginger.

golondrina candy-coated nut.

gordita round or oval appetizer of fried, usually stuffed *masa* (corn dough) covered with toppings. Typical stuffings are refried beans and *chicharrón*, or fried pork rind. The appetizer can be made several ways. The dough can be fried first and then split to form a cavity for the filling. Some puff up during frying, creating a pocket for fillings. Alternatively, a depression in an uncooked dough ball can be stuffed with filling and then closed by pinching the dough together. It is then fried in oil (also see *Menu Guide*).

granada pomegranate.

granada China Chinese granadilla, an ovoid yellow-skinned fruit of the passionfruit family with many seeds encased in white pulp.

granulado granulated sugar.

grasa fat; grease.

guajalote indigenous word for turkey; the Spanish, *pavo,* is used less often.

guaje flat, green seeds in long green or red-maroon tree-grown pods. The seeds are eaten raw or pulverized to make a sauce called *guasmole.*

guajillo see *chile guajillo.*

guajilote fruit, about 5 inches long and 2 inches wide, resembling a cucumber. Edible when yellow, it is eaten cooked or raw.

guanábana soursop, an asymmetrically heart-shaped, dark-green fruit up to 12 inches long with skin bearing many soft short projections.

guasmole see *guaje.*

guauzontle see *huauzontle.*

guavina small, dark brown river fish from Veracruz.

guayaba guava.

guayabate fruit paste or *ate* made from guava (*guayaba*).

güero see *chile güero.*

guía squash vine runner.

guisado cooked with seasonings.

guiso seasoning.

gusano de maguey worm from agave (*maguey*) plant leaves. Some *mezcal* producers include one in each bottle. They also are dried and used to flavor food. In Oaxaca they are doused with chile powder and salt before drying.

haba yellow fava bean.

habanero see *chile habanero.*

harina flour; wheat flour is *harina integral.*

hecho en casa homemade.

helado ice cream.

hierba herb; also spelled *yerba.*

hierba buena mint; also spelled *yerba buena.*

hierba de conejo rabbit herb used to flavor beans and rice.

hierba santa see *hoja santa*.

hierbas de olor sprigs of marjoram, thyme and oregano bundled together with bay leaves in an herb bouquet used in cooking.

hígado liver; also called *azadura*.

higo fig.

hinojo fennel.

hoja leaf.

hoja de aguacate avocado leaf used as a seasoning, either fresh or dried. It imparts an anise flavor to a dish.

hoja de maíz corn husk used fresh or dried to wrap *tamales*.

hoja de plátano banana leaf used to wrap food, especially in the Yucatán.

hoja santa soft, heart-shaped green leaf with anise-like flavor, used fresh as a wrapper for *tamales* or fish, and to season sauces, especially in Veracruz. Also known as *hierba santa, acuyo, tlanepa* and *momo*.

hoja verde de maíz leaf of the corn plant. It is used to wrap *corundas,* the unfilled, irregular-shaped *tamales* of Michoacán. Also called *hoja de milpa*.

hojaldra specialty bread of Etla, Oaxaca, which is *empanada*-shaped and drizzled with red-colored sugar.

hongo wild mushroom.

huachinango red snapper; *jalapeño* chiles with scale marks on the skin are called *huachinango*.

huarache large, oval snack made with *masa,* or corn dough (see *Menu Guide*).

huauzontle wild, broccoli-flavored plant with small green seeds; it is related to *amaranto* (this *Guide*). Also spelled *guauzontle*.

huevos eggs.

huevos batidos beaten eggs that are fried without stirring, as opposed to scrambled eggs, which are stirred during cooking.

huevos crudos raw eggs.

huevos de faltriquera a cinnamon-flavored sweet made of egg yolks and confectioner's sugar.

huevos estrellados eggs sunny side up; also called *huevos fritos estrellados*.

huevos hervidos duros hard-boiled eggs.

huevos tibios soft-boiled eggs.

huiche a zucchini-type squash local to Oaxaca.

huitlacoche see *cuitlacoche*.

ibes small, white beans grown in the Yucatán.

itacate food to go.

jabalí wild pig indigenous to the Yucatán.

jaibas small, hard-shelled crabs that usually end up in soup. In markets several typically are banded together with reeds.

jalapeño see *chile jalapeño.*

jalea jelly.

jamaica outermost flower parts, or sepals, of the hibiscus, which are used to make a drink called *agua de jamaica* (see *Menu Guide*).

jamón ham.

japonés *chile japonés;* see *chile serrano.*

jaqueton local name for black-finned shark in Campeche; it is used to make the popular dish called *pan de cazón* (see *Menu Guide*).

jarál *chile jarál;* see *chile* Poblano.

jengibre ginger.

jícama light-brown tuber with crispy, white flesh, which is sweet when fresh. It typically is eaten raw. Hefty sliced rounds are often sold by fruit vendors.

jícara gourd.

jitomate tomato; also called *tomate rojo.*

jobo plum-like fruit, often candied.

jocoque sour cream.

jugo juice.

jumiles pine beetles, found in Guerrero and Oaxaca. They are ground and added to chile sauces or eaten live as a *taco* filling.

kabik spicy broth.

kol white sauce.

langosta lobster.

langostino crayfish; also called *acamaya, camarones del río* and *cucaracha* (literally cockroach). Called *camaya* in Veracruz and Hidalgo, and *pigua* in Tabasco. Also see *acosil.*

laurel bay leaf.

lec dried gourd used to keep *tortillas* warm.

leche milk.

leche de cabra goat's milk.

leche de vaca cow's milk.

leche quemada milk that has been burned to produce a caramel taste.

lechecilla custard filling.

lechuga lettuce.

legumbre vegetable; also called *verdura*.

lengua tongue.

lenguado flounder or sole.

levadura yeast.

licuado water- or milk-based drink of puréed fruit pulp, made in a blender; also called *preparadora*.

licuadora blender.

liebre hare; large member of the rabbit family.

lima sweet lime. Considered a variety of small lemon, it is also called *limón*.

lima agria small, green, bitter lime with a nipple at one end. It is an important ingredient in Yucatecan dishes.

limón lemon.

limón relleno de coco a hollowed out candied lime filled with shredded coconut. Also called *dulce de limón*.

limonada lemonade; in restaurants, it can be made with sparkling water.

lisa salted, dried mullet popular in the Isthmus of Tehuantepec, Oaxaca, especially during Lent and Christmas.

lobina striped bass; black bass is called *lobina negra*.

lomo tenderloin. Also called *lomito*.

lonche lunch.

lonchería lunch counter.

longaniza type of *chorizo* made in one long strip rather than individual links. A pepperoni-like sausage of the same name is available in the Yucatán.

macarrón macaroni; also the name of a milk-based candy popular in Puebla, formed in a bar about 3 inches long with ridged surfaces.

machaca see *carne machaca*.

machacado crushed; shredded.

machines toasted, raw garbanzo beans still in the pod, a specialty of Tlacolula, Oaxaca.

maciza see *carne maciza*.

madura ripe.

maguey succulent agave or century plant, of great importance in Mexico long before the Spanish conquistadors arrived. It is the source of several drinks: *aguamiel,* the plant juice; *pulque,* a naturally fermented beer-like beverage made from the plant juice; and a stronger alcoholic beverage, *mezcal* (also see *tequila,* this *Guide*). The plant's heart, that which is left after all the spiked leaves, or *pencas,* are chopped off, can be eaten when roasted—

the first step in the fermentation process. Whole leaves are used to line barbecue pits and to wrap meats barbecued in these pits. Individual-size portions are wrapped in the skin of the leaves (*mixiote*). Plant fibers are used for weaving.

maguey cocido cooked fibrous heart of the *maguey* plant. Pieces are chewed to extract the meaty pulp and the remaining fiber is spit out. One can also hold a piece by the teeth and pull the fibers out of the mouth. Also called *maguey horneado,* or baked *maguey.*

maíz dried corn, as opposed to *elote,* or fresh corn.

maíz machacado hominy. It is made from a variety of large-kerneled white corn (*cacahuazintle*), which is boiled with slaked lime and then washed. Hulls become loosened and are easily removed by rubbing the kernels together. The germ at the kernel's base is removed by hand, allowing the kernel to "flower" when simmered in water.

maíz palomero unpopped popcorn.

mamey oval fruit with tan skin and orange flesh. Its large seed is ground and used to make the drink *tejate.* Also called *zapote rojo.*

manchamanteles see *mole manchamanteles.*

mandarina tangerine.

mango de oro large red or greenish-red mango; also called *petacón.*

mango manila small, very sweet yellow mango.

manitas de cangrejo stone crab; pig's feet are *manitas de cerdo.*

mano name for the foot of an animal, after butchering; also see *metate.*

mantaraya tropical ray, or skate.

manteca lard; also called *manteca de cerdo* and *manteca de puerco.*

mantequilla butter.

marañón cashew apple.

mariscos seafood.

marquesote type of bread cake topped with powdered sugar; can also be used to make a syrup-soaked dessert called *ante* (see *Menu Guide*).

masa corn dough made from dried field corn that has been boiled in slaked lime to facilitate removal of the tough hulls. Treated corn is ground into dough for *tortillas, tamales* and various appetizers, or *antojitos.* Dough is made from red, blue, white and yellow varieties of corn.

masa harina fresh *masa* (corn dough) that has been dried and ground.

media cooked medium (meat).

médula marrow.

mejorana marjoram.

melado cane sugar syrup. In Nayarit it typically is mixed with cottage cheese.

melaza molasses; also called *miel de sorgo.*

melón melon other than watermelon.

membrillo quince; candy paste made from quince is *membrillate*.

memela see *sope*.

merienda late afternoon snack, partaken more typically in urban settings.

mermelada marmalade or jam.

mero grouper.

metate small, three-legged rectangular work table with an inclined surface. Made of basalt, it is used to grind corn, chiles and ingredients for sauces, or *moles,* including roasted *cacao* beans. An elongated basalt stone called a *mano* or *metlapil* is used to grind food on it.

metlapil see *metate*.

mezcal liquor distilled from the heart, or *piña,* of the agave (*maguey*) plant, typically from the species *Agave augustifolia*. It is manufactured by hand in villages, especially in the Oaxaca Valley.

miel honey, syrup and molasses.

miel de abeja honey from bees.

miel de sorgo molasses; also called *melaza*.

migada see *sope*.

miltomate see *tomate*.

mirasol see *chile mirasol*.

mixiote tough but pliable skin from the spiked leaves of the agave (*maguey*) plant, which is used like parchment to wrap seasoned meats for cooking. It is carefully removed from the leaf by hand, using a sharp knife.

mojarra small, silvery, large-eyed tropical fish.

molcajete three-legged basalt mortar used to grind spices and chiles for sauces with a pestle called a *tejolote*. The mortar typically becomes a serving bowl for the sauces made in it.

mole rich-flavored complex sauce made with any of several combinations of ground nuts and seeds, chiles, spices, dried fruits, dried aromatic leaves, chocolate and *masa* (corn dough).

mole adobo vinegary, seasoned red chile sauce.

mole amarillo light red-orange sauce, traditionally made with yellow *chilhaucle* and reddish-brown *chilcostle* chiles, tomatillos, herbs and spices. One of Oaxaca's seven most famous *moles* (see *Menu Guide*). Also simply called *amarillo*.

mole chichilo complex sauce of spices, seeds, dried fruit and nuts, flavored and colored by blackened seeds of the *chilhuacle negro* and *guajillo* chiles, and burned *tortillas*. One of Oaxaca's seven most famous *moles* (see *Menu Guide*). Also called *chichilo* Oaxaqueño or simply *chichilo*.

mole coloradito complex, rich, red sauce of *ancho* and *guajillo* chiles, spices, nuts, seeds, raisins and chocolate. One of Oaxaca's seven most famous *moles* (see *Menu Guide*). Also simply called *coloradito*.

mole colorado complex brick-red sauce made with *pasilla, mulato* and *chilhuacle rojo* chiles, tomatillos, herbs, seeds, nuts, raisins and spices. One of Oaxaca's seven most famous *moles* (see *Menu Guide*). Also called *mole rojo* or simply *colorado.*

mole de almendra almond sauce with herbs and spices (see *Menu Guide*). Also simply called *almendrado.*

mole manchamanteles red sauce made with *ancho* chiles, herbs, spices, sweet potatoes, fresh pineapple and plantains. One of Oaxaca's seven most famous *moles* (see *Menu Guide*). The name means "tablecloth stainer," and the sauce does indeed do that. Also simply called *manchamanteles.*

mole negro complex black sauce made with *mulato, pasilla* and *chilhuacle negro* chiles, tomatillos, herbs, nuts, seeds, spices, chocolate, bananas, and blackened *tortillas* and chile seeds for color and additional flavor. One of Oaxaca's seven most famous *moles* (see *Menu Guide*).

mole rojo see *mole colorado.*

mole verde green sauce made of tomatillos, fresh *jalapeño* or *serrano* chiles, cilantro, parsley and herbs called *epazote* and *hoja santa,* thickened with *masa* (corn dough). One of Oaxaca's seven most famous *moles* (see *Menu Guide*). Also simply called *verde.*

molida ground.

molinillo hand-carved wooden rotary whisk used to make a thick layer of foam on top of hot chocolate; it was a Spanish contribution to the Mexican kitchen. The Aztecs made their coveted chocolate foam by pouring the beverage from a vessel held several feet above the receiving one.

molito *mole,* or sauce, made with dried or fresh fish; made in the Isthmus of Tehuantepec, Oaxaca.

momo see *hoja santa.*

mondongo intestines; tripe.

morcilla blood sausage. In Valladolid, Yucatán, it also contains brains and is seasoned with *recado negro,* a seasoning paste of spices and charred chiles. Also called *rellena.*

Moreliana pastry-like *tortilla* topped with milk-based candy, a specialty of Morelia, Michoacán.

Moreliana de cacahuate peanut brittle, a treat from Morelia, Michoacán.

Moreliano see *ate.*

morita see *chile morita.*

moronga sausage made of pork blood using the large intestines of the pig.

moyo large crab popular in Michoacán and Colima.

mueganos deep-fried snack made of pieces of flour and molasses dough formed into a ball held together with crystallized sugar.

mueganos de vino strips of wine-containing dough, colored yellow and fried. The strips are then sprinkled with wine and topped with sugar syrup and fondant. It is a treat from Puebla.

mulato see *chile mulato*.

nabo turnip.

nacidos bean sprouts.

nanche yellow chokecherry.

naranja orange (the fruit and the color); the fruit is *chino* in the Yucatán.

naranja agria the bitter Seville orange. It is used in many Yucatecan dishes and for marmalade.

nata clotted cream.

negro black; also the name for a small, shiny black bean.

nicuatole white, gelatin-like *atole* made of *masa* (corn dough), sugar and water. This preparation of Tlacolula is sold in blocks with two red sides.

nieve ice made with flavored water; sherbet.

nixtamal dried corn that has been boiled in slaked lime but has not yet been ground into wet *masa* (corn dough).

nogada sauce made of ground walnuts and spices.

nopal succulent, paddle-shaped leaf of the cactus of the same name, cooked and eaten as a vegetable after the sharp spines are cut off. Also called a *nopalito*. Another name for this cactus is the prickly pear.

nopales cocidos boiled cactus paddles.

nuevo new.

nuez nut.

nuez cáscara de papel pecan; also called *nuez encarcelada*.

nuez de Castilla walnut.

nuez moscada nutmeg.

obleas sandwich cookie made of two thin wafers with a caramel filling called *cajeta* (see this *Guide*).

oferta on sale. A synonym is *ganga*.

olla round-bottomed, large-necked clay cooking pot with two handles.

ostión oyster.

pagua large variety of avocado with hard green skin.

palanqueta peanut brittle-like candy made with peanuts or pumpkin seeds.

paleta fruit popsicle; can also be a lollipop.

palomitas popped popcorn.

pambazo soft, round bun; also a sandwich (see *Menu Guide*).

pan bread.

pan blanco oval specialty roll used in Puebla to make the sandwich called *chanclas* (see *Menu Guide*).

pan de anise muffin-sized sweet bread coated with sugar and flavored with anise; this specialty of Pátzcuaro, Michoacán, can also consist of two small balls of baked dough held together by a filling.

pan de cazuela sweet, cinnamon bread cooked in a small *cazuela,* or cooking pan. The dough is coiled as it is put into the pan, giving the baked bread a snail shell appearance. It is a specialty of Tlacolula, Oaxaca.

pan de muerto special bread made for The Day of the Dead celebration. It is decorated with dough "bones" radiating out from a central "knob" representing the skull.

pan de yema egg bread, typically eaten with chocolate on special occasions.

pan dulce sweet roll.

pan Francés see *bolillo.*

pan tostado toast.

panadería bakery.

panela unrefined sugar formed into a loaf or brick; it can also be called *piloncillo,* the name more often used for a cone-shaped piece of unrefined sugar. Also the name for a type of cheese (see *queso panela*).

panocha see *piloncillo.*

panza beef tripe.

papa potato.

papa de agua water potato, a finger-sized red potato with crisp, juicy flesh.

papaloquelite pungent wild herb with large round leaves used as a garnish; also simply called *pápalo.*

papita del monte small, wild potato from San Luis Potosí.

pargo porgy, a type of snapper.

parrilla a grill.

pasa raisin.

pasilla see *chile pasilla.*

pastel cake.

pastelería pastry shop.

pata foot or hock; beef hock is *pata de res.*

pavo turkey; also called *guajolote.*

pay pie.

pechuga breast meat.

pejelagarto garfish; smoked *pejelagarto* is popular in Tabasco.

pelado peeled.

pellizcada see *sope*.

pelona round sandwich roll with crackled surface; also the name of a specialty sandwich in Puebla (see *Menu Guide*).

penca spiked leaf of the agave (*maguey*) plant.

pepicha herb with strong cilantro-like flavor.

pepino cucumber.

pepita pumpkin seed; also a milk-based fudge from Puebla.

pepitoria brittle made with pumpkin seeds; it is a specialty of Michoacán.

pera pear.

perejíl parsley.

perifollo chervil.

perón *chile perón;* see *chile manzano.*

peruano light yellow bean.

pescado a fish when caught for food; live fish are called *pez.*

pescado blanco whitefish from Lake Pátzcuaro, Michoacán. Also called *blanco de Pátzcuaro.*

petacón large red or greenish-red mango; also called *mango de oro.*

pez live fish; also see *pescado.*

pib pit used to barbecue food in the Yucatán.

pibil Yucatecan-style pit barbecue; meats typically are covered in spice paste and wrapped in banana leaves.

pibinal pit-roasted ear of corn.

picada see *sope.*

picadillo seasoned ground or shredded meat with candied and dried fruit, used as a stuffing.

picado finely chopped.

picante spicy hot.

pichón pigeon; squab.

pierna leg.

pigua see *langostino.*

piloncillo unrefined sugar molded into cones; also called *panocha.*

pimentón cayenne pepper.

pimienta pepper.

pimienta blanca white pepper.

pimienta dulce allspice; also called *pimienta gorda* and *pimienta grande.*

pimienta negra black pepper.

pimiento morrón bell pepper; also called *chile dulce.*

piña pineapple; also the heart of the agave plant (see *maguey*).

pinoché see *arrayán*.

pinole powdered, toasted corn mixed with cinnamon and sugar; also a drink made of this corn powder mixed with milk or water.

piñón pine nut.

pinto spotted bean; also called *cabra*.

pipián sauce of ground pumpkin seeds, nuts and spices.

piquín see *chile* piquín.

pitahaya sweet, red cactus fruit with pink pulp and many tiny black seeds.

plátano banana.

plátano dominico a tiny, "finger" banana.

plátano macho plantain; black when ripe, this starchy fruit is always cooked.

plátano morado sweet maroon-colored variety of banana.

plátano prensado candy made of steamed plantains pressed into blocks.

Poblano see *chile* Poblano.

pollo chicken.

pollo deshebrado shredded chicken.

polvorón crumbly cookie sprinkled with powdered sugar. Traditionally wrapped in tissue paper twisted at each end and fringed.

ponche hot punch made with fruit; *mezcal,* sugar cane spirits (*aguardiente de caña*) or other alcohol can be added.

porro leek.

posta chop or thick slice of meat or fish.

postre dessert.

pox *aguardiente*-like brew made with sugar and corn; a regional specialty of Chiapas. Also the name of a tropical fruit (see *cherimoya*, this *Guide*).

pozol water-based drink of *masa* (corn dough) traditionally drunk out of cups made of gourds. It is a specialty of Tabasco.

preparadora see *licuado*.

primera cooked rare (meat).

puchas Zacatecanas a sweet made of of egg yolks, flour, orange juice and lard formed into balls and fried. They are then coated with sugar syrup and rolled in cinnamon; also called *puchas de canela*.

puerco pork.

pulpo octopus.

pulque somewhat chalky, beer-like beverage made from naturally fermented juice of the agave (*maguey*) plant, primarily the species *Agave salmiana*. Long before the Spanish Conquest this mildly alcoholic beverage was an important drink. A similar brew made from corn is called *sende*.

pulquería shop selling *pulque*.

pura carne see *carne maciza*.

quelite any edible wild green; lamb's quarters, or *quelite cenizo,* is the most commonly eaten.

quemado burned.

querepo small whitefish from Lake Pátzcuaro, Michoacán, fried and eaten whole.

quesadilla uncooked *tortilla* topped on one side with any number of fillings, then folded in half to form a turnover and sealed at the edges. It is then cooked on a *comal,* or griddle.

quesillo de Oaxaca Oaxacan soft, cooked white cheese pulled into long, 1-inch wide strands and rolled into balls. This cheese melts well and is often used in dishes with cheese stuffings, such as *quesadillas* and stuffed chiles. Also called *queso de* Oaxaca and simply *quesillo.*

queso cheese; *queso fresco* sometimes is simply called *queso.*

queso añejo non-melting, fresh cheese that has been salted, dried and used grated or crumbled as a garnish. When the surface of the cheese is coated with chile powder, the cheese is called *queso enchilada.* It is also called *queso oreado, queso seco, añejo de* Cotija, *queso de* Cotija, or simply Cotija, after the town in Michoacán where the cheese originated.

queso asadero soft and stringy, braided, melting cheese made in northern Mexico. It is melted directly on a griddle. Also simply called *asadero.* It is called *queso cocido* in Sonora.

queso Chihuahua mild, light-yellow, cheddar-like melting cheese often used grated as a garnish. This type of cheese, available in wheels or "logs," originated in the Mennonite community in Chihuahua.

queso cocido see *queso asadero.*

queso crema cream cheese.

queso de Apatzingán soft cheese made in Apatzingán, Michoacán, a city in the hot lands, or Tierra Caliente, between the central volcanic chain of mountains and the southern Sierra Madre range.

queso de Cotija see *queso añejo.*

queso de metate see *queso fresco.*

queso de Oaxaca see *quesillo de Oaxaca.*

queso de puerco head cheese. This regional pork product of Toluca, Mexico, is made of head meat pressed and sold in round, flattened woven cases.

queso de Tierra Caliente any of several hard cheeses made in the Tierra Caliente of Michoacán, the hot lands between the central volcanic chain of mountains and the southern Sierra Madre range.

queso de tuna a jelly-like confection made from cactus fruit juice. It is a specialty of Zacatecas.

queso enchilada see *queso añejo.*

queso fresco easily crumbled fresh, salty cheese. Also called *queso de metate* and simply *queso.*

queso manchego semi-firm, light-yellow cheese, sometimes aged, used for melting or as a topping.

queso oreado see *queso añejo.*

queso panela fresh, soft white cheese molded in a round, flat woven basket that leaves a pattern on the cheese.

queso ranchero fresh cheese similar to *queso fresco,* but the curds are broken up and remolded before packaging.

queso seco see *queso añejo.*

quintonil an edible herb.

rábano radish; horseradish is *rábano fuerte.*

rajas strips cut from toasted, skinned chiles.

rallado grated.

raspados flavored ices. Shavings from an ice block are topped with any of several syrup flavors.

rebanada a slice.

recado one of several types of Yucatecan prepared seasoning pastes. In the markets, each mixture is patted into a huge, showy mound, ready for shoppers to get a scoopful; some are also pre-packaged in cellophane.

recado de bistec Yucatecan spice paste made of garlic, spices and juice of the bitter Seville orange. It is used to flavor steak and to pickle dishes.

recado negro Yucatecan black spice paste made of blackened chiles, roasted onion and garlic, ground spices and juice from the bitter Seville orange. Also called *chirmole* and *chilmole.*

recado rojo brick-red Yucatecan spice paste made with ground *achiote* seeds, spices, garlic and vinegar. Meat or fish typically is covered with the paste and cooked in banana leaves. It is also used to flavor many dishes. Another name for the paste is *adobo de achiote.*

refresco soft drink; also called *gaseosa.*

rellena blood sausage; also called *morcilla.*

relleno stuffing.

rellenos de mariscos stuffed with seafood.

remolacha red beet; also called *betabel.*

repollo cabbage; more commonly called *col.*

requesón cheese resembling cottage cheese, made from whey.

res beef.

riñón kidney.

riñonada choice, lower part of the back of a *cabrito* (kid). It can include the kidneys and the associated fatty sheath.

róbalo snook, a fish related to the sea bass.

romeritos rosemary-like wild green, or *quelite,* with succulent leaves, used fresh or cooked. It is also the name of a Lenten dish of fritters with dried shrimp and *romerito* greens (see *Menu Guide*).

romero rosemary.

rompope eggnog-like liqueur made with egg yolks, a specialty of Puebla.

rosita de cacao flower used in making *tejate* (see this *Guide*).

sábalo milkfish.

sabino type of sweet tan or red-brown bean; also called *bayo.*

sal salt.

salchicha hot dog; also the name of a beef sausage.

salchichón type of large sausage.

salpicón dish of shredded fish, seafood or meat.

salsa table sauce; the simplest ones contain chopped tomato, or tomatillo, onion, garlic, chiles and cilantro. The piquancy depends on the chiles used.

salsa arriera "muledrivers' sauce," a very hot, thick mixture made with *serrano* chiles, onion and garlic.

salsa borracha "drunken" chile sauce made with *pulque,* the fermented sap of the agave (*maguey*) plant. It typically accompanies a barbecue (*barbacoa*).

salsa cocida de jitomate cooked sauce made with puréed tomatoes, green chiles, garlic and onions.

salsa cruda see *salsa* Mexicana.

salsa de cacahuate peanut sauce.

salsa de chile chipotle y jitomate sauce made with toasted *chipotle* chiles and roasted tomatoes.

salsa de jitomate del norte mild tomato and chile sauce of northern Mexico.

salsa de molcajete coarse, uncooked sauce made with the traditional three-legged mortar (*molcajete*) and pestle (*tejolote*).

salsa de tomate verde cocida sauce of tomatillos and green chiles.

salsa endiablada deviled sauce of chiles, spices and cider vinegar.

salsa fresca see *salsa* Mexicana.

salsa Huichol sauce made of *cascabel* chiles, spices, vinegar and salt.

salsa Mexicana uncooked sauce of tomatoes, onions, green chiles and cilantro. Also called *salsa* Mexicana *cruda, salsa cruda* and *salsa fresca.*

salsa ranchera tomato, onion and hot green chile sauce.

salsa Veracruzana sauce of tomatoes, olives, *jalapeño* chiles, and capers.

salsa verde cruda uncooked green sauce made with green chiles, onions, cilantro and cooked tomatillos.

sandía watermelon.

seco dry.

semilla seed.

semilla de cilantro cilantro seed, or coriander.

semilla de girasol sunflower seed.

sencillo simple.

sende see *pulque.*

serrano see *chile serrano.*

servilleta napkin.

sesos brains.

shote freshwater snail.

sierra mackerel.

sin without.

sin gas without carbonation.

sin grasa without fat.

sopa soup.

sopa aguada "wet," or brothy soup; compare with *sopa seca,* or dry soup.

sopa seca "dry" soup; rice or pasta dishes are considered dry soups because they start out soupy but absorb all the broth when cooked; they are served before the main course. Compare with *sopa aguada,* or "wet" soup, which has ingredients in broth, or liquid.

sope appetizer made from a thick, cooked *tortilla* pinched up around the edge to form a rim to contain a savory topping, then baked on a *comal,* or griddle, when filled. Not surprisingly, many regional names and toppings exist. A round one can be a *picada, garnacha, bocol, migada* or *pellizcada.* An oval one, formed by flattening a cylinder rather than a ball of dough, can be a *memela* or *chalupa* (also see *Menu Guide*).

surtido an assortment.

taco soft (unfried) corn *tortilla* rolled around a filling; called *taco dorado* if it is fried.

taco de harina soft wheat flour *tortilla* rolled around a filling; also see *burra.*

tallarín noodle.

tamal *masa* (corn dough) blended with lard until light, and steamed in corn husks, banana leaves or corn leaves. Traditionally, the corn used is *cacahuazintle,* a large-kerneled white corn also used to make hominy. This special-occasion food made without lard was on menus long before the Conquest. Most are served without sauce.

taquería taco stand.

tasajo In Oaxaca, beef *cecina.* It is used fresh, marinated and salted, or aged in salt to make a type of jerky; see *cecina.*

taza cup.

té tea.

té de damiana tea brewed with *damiana,* an aromatic desert herb.

té de manzanilla camomile tea.

té limón lemon grass tea.

té negro black tea.

tejate drink made of *masa* (corn dough), ground local *cacao* beans, *mamey* seeds, grated coconut, granulated sugar, water and a flower called *rosita de cacao.* Traditionally it is drunk out of a small, colorfully painted bowl made from a gourd. Also spelled *texate.*

tejocote small, yellow-orange fruit like a crab apple; it is a typical punch, or *ponche,* ingredient.

tejolote see *molcajete.*

tejuino drink made with fermented corn and unrefined sugar.

telera flat, oblong bread roll with two characteristic grooves in the surface; used to make a *torta* (see this *Guide*).

tenedor fork.

tepache fermented drink made of pineapple and unrefined sugar.

tepescuintle agouti, a rabbit-like rodent especially enjoyed in Tabasco.

tequesquite natural salt used as a leavening agent.

tequila type of *mezcal* distilled from the juice of the agave plant, using cultivated varieties of the species *Agave tequilina,* especially the "blue agave." The hub of *tequila* production is Tequila, Jalisco. *Sangrita,* made with chile sauce and tomato, orange and lime juice, is the typical chaser.

ternera veal.

tescalate drink made with ground beans and toasted corn, seasoned with *achiote.* It is a specialty of Chiapas.

tiburón dogfish or small shark; also called *cazón.*

tienda small grocery store.

tierno tender.

tinga spicy meat mixture originating in Puebla.

tlanepa see *hoja santa.*

tlatloyo oval-shaped appetizer made with blue or yellow *masa* (corn dough). Also spelled *tlacoyo*.

tlayuda Oaxacan foot-wide *tostada,* also spelled *clayuda.*

tobala expensive *mezcal* made from a rare, wild variety of agave (*maguey*) plant, distilled in black ceramic containers.

tocino bacon.

tomate tomatillo, an acidic, light green or purple tomato-like fruit covered with a paper husk, which is removed before cooking. Also called *tomate verde.* Other names for tomatillo are *miltomate* and *milpa verde* because it grows wild in the cornfield, or *milpa. Tomate manzano* is a larger, sweeter variety that grows in Toluca, Mexico.

tomate rojo tomato; also called *jitomate.*

tomillo thyme.

toronja grapefruit.

torta Mexico's super sandwich stuffed with many layers of different ingredients, typically in a *telera* (see this *Guide*). Also the name for sweet and savory cakes.

torta de huevo omelette.

tortilla thin circle of fresh *masa* (corn dough) made from dried corn kernels boiled in water and slaked lime to loosen the hull, and cooked on a *comal,* or griddle.

tortilla de agua huge—up to 2 feet in diameter—thin, wheat flour *tortilla* that is folded twice, like a napkin, and eaten like bread. This specialty of Hermosilla, Sonora, is also called *tortilla de sobaco,* or armpit, because the elastic dough used to make it extends to the armpit as it is slapped back and forth between the hands.

tortilla de harina de trigo wheat flour *tortilla.*

tortilla de masa harina *tortilla* made from reconstituted dried *masa* (corn dough).

tortilla de sobaco see *tortilla de agua.*

tortita fritter; also called *fritura.*

tortuga turtle; also called *caguama.* Many types of turtle are endangered.

tostada crispy, fried *tortilla* garnished with any of several toppings. Oaxaca has a large, foot-wide one (*tlayuda*).

tostadita fried piece of *tortilla.*

totomoxtle corn husk.

totopo *tortilla* cut into pieces, fried to a crisp and used as a garnish or edible tableware. It also is the name for a crunchy *tortilla* made from fresh corn. Small holes are made in it to facilitate its removal from the walls of the tandor-like oven in which it is baked. This specialty *tortilla* is from the Isthmus of Tehuantepec, Oaxaca.

trigo wheat.

trucha trout.

trucha ahumada smoked trout.

tuba fermented sap from the coconut palm.

tuna prickly pear, the magenta or green oval fruit of the nopal cactus.

tuna agria see *xoconostle.*

turrón nougat.

uchepo fresh corn *tamal* of Michoacán, wrapped in a leaf of the corn plant.

uva grape.

vaso glass.

venado venison.

verde green; also see *mole verde.*

verdolagas the herb purslane.

verdura vegetable; also called *legumbre.*

vinagre vinegar.

xcat-ik see *chile güero.*

xoconostle fruit from a cactus related to prickly pear; it is smaller and sourer than *tuna,* the fruit of the prickly pear cactus; also called *tuna agria.*

xonequi heart-shaped wild green native to Veracruz.

xtabentún Yucatecan liquor made of fermented honey flavored with anise.

yema yolk.

yerba herb; also spelled *hierba.*

yerba buena mint; also spelled *hierba buena.*

zanahoria carrot.

zapote negro black sapodilla, a green tropical fruit with sweet, dark-brown to black pulp.

zapote rojo oval fruit with tan skin and orange flesh; also called *mamey.*

zempasúchil bright orange marigold, whose petals are fed to chickens in some regions of Mexico to make their skin yellow. The flowers traditionally are used to decorate graves on The Day of the Dead.

Bibliography

Atkinson, Sonja G. *The Aztec Way to Healthy Eating*. New York: Paragon House, 1992.

Bayless, Rick with Deann Groen Bayless. *Authentic Mexican: Regional Cooking from the Heart of Mexico*. New York: William Morrow and Company, Inc., 1987.

Bayless, Rick with Deann Groen Bayless and JeanMarie Brownson. *Rick Bayless's Mexican Kitchen: Capturing the Vibrant Flavors of a World-Class Cuisine*. New York: Scribner, 1996.

Benítez, Ana M. de. *Pre-Hispanic Cooking*, 2nd edition. Mexico: Ediciones Euroamericanas Klaus Thiele, 1976.

Blue, Betty A. *Authentic Mexican Cooking: Auténtica Cocina de Méjico*. Englewood Cliffs, New Jersey: Prentice-Hall, Inc., 1977.

Boone, Elizabeth Hill. *The Aztec World*. Montreal: St. Remy Press; Washington, DC: Smithsonian Books, 1994.

Booth, George C. *The Food and Drink of Mexico*. New York: Dover Publications, Inc., 1976.

Brosnahan, Tom. *Guatemala, Belize & Yucatán: La Ruta Maya*, 2nd edition. Australia: Lonely Planet Publications, 1994.

Cadwallader, Sharon. *Savoring Mexico: A Travel Cookbook*. New York: McGraw-Hill Book Company, 1980.

Cantrell, Jacqueline Phillips. *Ancient Mexico: Cultural Traditions in the Land of the Feathered Serpent,* 2nd edition. Dubuque, Iowa: Kendall/Hunt Publishers, 1986.

Carrasco, Davíd. *Religions of Mesoamerica: Cosmovision and Ceremonial Centers*. San Francisco: Harper and Row, 1990.

Coe, Michael D. *Mexico: From the Olmecs to the Aztecs,* 4th edition. London: Thames and Hudson, 1994.

Coe, Michael, Dean Snow and Elizabeth Benson. *Atlas of Ancient America*. New York: Facts on File Publications, 1986.

Coe, Sophie D. *America's First Cuisines*. Austin, Texas: University of Texas Press, 1994.

Coe, Sophie D. and Michael D. Coe. *The True History of Chocolate*. New York: Thames and Hudson, 1996.

Crosby, Alfred W. Jr. *The Columbian Exchange: Biological and Cultural Consequences of 1492.* Westport, Connecticut: Greenwood Publishing Company, 1972.

Davies, Nigel. *The Ancient Kingdoms of Mexico.* London: Allen Lane, 1982.

Díaz del Castillo, Bernal. *The Discovery and Conquest of Mexico: 1517–1521,* edited by Genaro García and translated by A.P. Maudslay. New York: Noonday Press, 1956.

Ebeling, Walter. *Handbook of Indian Foods and Fibers of Arid America.* Berkeley, California: University of California Press, 1986.

Farga, Amando. *Historia de la Comida en Mexico.* Mexico D.F., Mexico: Costa-Amic, 1968.

Fernández, Adela. *Traditional Mexican Cooking and Its Best Recipes.* Mexico City: Panorama Editorial, S.A. de C.V., 1997.

Franz, Carl. *The People's Guide to Mexico,* 8th edition. Santa Fe, New Mexico: John Muir Publications, 1990.

Hamblin, Nancy L. *Animal Use by the Cozumel Maya.* Tucson, Arizona: The University of Arizona Press, 1984.

Horcasitas, Fernando. *The Aztecs Then and Now.* Mexico City: Editorial Minutiae Mexicana, S.A. de C.V., 1979.

Hutson, Lucinda. *¡Tequila! Cooking with the Spirit of Mexico.* Berkeley, California: Ten Speed Press, 1995.

Idell, Albert, editor and translator. *The Bernal Díaz Chronicles: The True Story of the Conquest of Mexico.* Garden City, New York: Dolphin Books, 1956.

Kelley, David Humiston. *Deciphering the Maya Script.* Austin, Texas: University of Texas Press, 1976.

Kennedy, Diana. *The Cuisines of Mexico.* New York: Harper & Row, Publishers, 1972.

Kennedy, Diana. *The Art of Mexican Cooking: Traditional Mexican Cooking for Aficionados.* New York: Bantam Books, 1989.

Kennedy, Diana. *Mexican Regional Cooking,* Revised Edition. New York: Harper Perennial, 1990.

Kerr, W. Park and Norma Kerr. *The El Paso Chile Company's Texas Border Cookbook.* New York: William Morrow and Company, Inc., 1992.

Klor de Alva, J. Jorge, H.B. Nicholson and Eloise Quiñones Keber, editors. *The Work of Bernardino de Sahagun: Pioneer Ethnographer of Sixteenth-Century Aztec Mexico,* volume II. Albany, New York: Institute for Mesoamerican Studies, 1988.

Kraig, Bruce and Dudley Nieto. *Cuisines of Hidden Mexico: A Culinary Journey to Guerrero and Michoacán.* New York: John Wiley & Sons, Inc., 1996.

Lameiras, Brigitte Boehm de. *Comer y Vivir en Guadalajara: Divertimento Histórico-Culinario.* Zamora, Michoacán, Mexico: El Colegio de Michoacán; Guadalajara, Jalisco, Mexico: Secretaría de Cultura de Jalisco, El Colegio de Jalisco, Sociedad Siglo XXI, 1996.

Martínez, Zarela. *The Food and Life of Oaxaca: Traditional Recipes from Mexico's Heart.* New York: MacMillan, 1997.

Martínez, Zarela. *Food from My Heart: Cuisines of Mexico Remembered and Reimagined.* New York: Macmillan, 1992.

Mendelsohn, Lotte. *Healthy Mexican Regional Cookery: A Culinary Travelogue.* Weston, Massachusetts: Font & Center Press, 1995.

Morton, Lyman. *Yucatán Cookbook: Recipes & Tales.* Santa Fe, New Mexico: Red Crane Books, 1996.

Novo, Salvador. *Cocina Mexicana o Historia Gastronomica de La Ciudad de Mexico.* Mexico: Editorial Porrua, S.A., 1967.

Ortiz, Elisabeth Lambert. *The Complete Book of Mexican Cooking.* New York, M. Evans and Company, Inc., 1967.

Palazuelos, Susanna and Marilyn Tausend. *Mexico the Beautiful Cookbook.* San Francisco, California: Collins Publishers, 1994.

Quintana, Patricia with Jack Bishop. *Cuisine of the Water Gods: The Authentic Seafood and Vegetable Cookery of Mexico.* New York: Simon & Schuster, 1994.

Quintana, Patricia with Carol Haralson. *Mexico's Feasts of Life.* Tulsa, Oklahoma: Council Oak Books, 1994.

Roberts, Timothy R. *Myths of the World: Gods of the Maya, Aztecs and Incas.* New York: Friedman/Fairfax Publishers, 1996.

Rosa, Angeles de la and C. Gandia de Fernández. *Flavors of Mexico: Authentic Recipes from South of the Border.* San Ramon, California: 101 Productions, 1978.

Sahagún, Fray Bernardino de. *Florentine Codex: General History of the Things of New Spain,* edited and translated by Arthur J.O. Anderson and Charles E. Dibble, book VIII, *Kings and Lords.* Utah: The School of American Research and The University of Utah; Santa Fe, New Mexico: Monographs of The School of American Research, 1954.

Sahagún, Fray Bernardino de. *Florentine Codex: General History of the Things of New Spain,* edited and translated by Arthur J.O. Anderson and Charles E. Dibble, book IX, *The Merchants.* Utah: The School of American Research and The University of Utah; Santa Fe, New Mexico: Monographs of The School of American Research and The Museum of New Mexico, 1959.

Soustelle, Jacques. *Daily Life of the Aztecs.* Stanford, California: Stanford University Press, 1970.

Super, John C. *Food, Conquest, and Colonization in Sixteenth-Century Spanish America.* Albuquerque, New Mexico: University of New Mexico Press, 1988.

Tannahill, Reay. *Food in History.* New York: Stein and Day, 1973.

Taube, Karl. *The Legendary Past: Aztec and Maya Myths.* London: British Museum Press; Austin, Texas, University of Texas Press, 1993.

Tausend, Marilyn with Miguel Ravago. *Cocina de la Familia: More Than 200 Authentic Recipes from Mexican-American Home Kitchens.* New York: Simon & Schuster, 1997.

Torres Yzábal, María Dolores and Shelton Wiseman. *The Mexican Gourmet: Authentic Ingredients and Traditional Recipes from the Kitchens of Mexico.* San Diego, California: Thunder Bay Press, 1995.

Wauchope, Robert, editor. *Handbook of Middle American Indians,* volumes 7 and 8, Ethnology, parts 1 and 2. Austin, Texas: University of Texas Press, 1969.

Velázquez de León, Josefina. *Mexican Cook Book Devoted to American Homes.* Bilingual edition with English translation by Concepción Silva Garcia. Mexico City: Ediciones Velázquez de León, 1947.

Zaslavsky, Nancy. *A Cook's Tour of Mexico: Authentic Recipes from the Country's Best Open-Air Markets, City Fondas, and Home Kitchens.* New York: St. Martin's Griffin, 1995.

Index

ORDER FORM

Use this form to order additional copies of *Eat Smart in Mexico: How to Decipher the Menu, Know the Market Foods and Embark on a Tasting Adventure,* or to order any of the other guidebooks in the EAT SMART series.

Please send me:

_____ **Eat Smart in Mexico (2nd Edition)** - $13.95

_____ **Eat Smart in Sicily** - $13.95

_____ **Eat Smart in Peru** - $13.95

_____ **Eat Smart in Brazil (2nd Edition)** - $13.95

_____ **Eat Smart in Turkey (2nd Edition)** - $13.95

_____ **Eat Smart in India** - $13.95

_____ **Eat Smart in Morocco** - $12.95

_____ **Eat Smart in Poland** - $12.95

_____ **Eat Smart in Indonesia** - $12.95

Add $3.00 postage for one book, $1.00 for each additional book. Wisconsin residents add 5% sales tax. For international orders, please inquire about postal charges.

Check enclosed for $ _____

Name: _____

Address: _____

City: _____ State: _____ Zip: _____

Telephone: _____

Email: _____

Mail this form to:

 GINKGO PRESS
P.O. Box 5346
Madison, WI 53705
Tel: 608-233-5488 • Fax: 608-233-0053
www.ginkgopress.com • info@ginkgopress.com

design Ekeby
cover design Susan P. Chwae
color separations Traver Graphics, Inc.
printing Malloy, Inc.

typefaces Garamond Simoncini and Helvetica Black
paper 60# Thor